TEXTILES

A Norton Professional Book

Revised Edition

TEXTILES
A Handbook for Designers

Marypaul Yates

W.W. Norton & Company
New York • London

For Benjamin
with love yesterday, and today, in all editions

Copyright © 1996, 1986 by Marypaul Yates

For information about permission to reproduce selections from this book, write to Permissions, W. W. Norton & Company, Inc., 500 Fifth Avenue, New York, NY 10110.

The text of this book is composed in Times Roman with the display set in Helvetica
Color printed by Brady-Palmer Printing Company
Manufacturing by Edwards Brothers, Inc.
Cover illustration: Tapestry floral. (GA. Peach Designs. Photo: Maryanne Solensky)

Library of Congress Cataloging-in-Publication Data

Yates, Marypaul.
Textiles : a handbook for designers / Marypaul Yates. —Rev. ed.
         p.   cm.
    "A Norton professional book."
    Includes bibliographical references and index.
    ISBN 0-393-73003-4 (pbk.)
    1. Textile design.   I. Title.
TS1475.Y37   1995
677'.022—dc20   95-33007
                                                            CIP
                                                            rev.

ISBN 0-393-73003-4 (pbk.)

W. W. Norton & Company, Inc., 500 Fifth Avenue, New York, NY 10110
W. W. Norton & Company Ltd., 10 Coptic Street, London WC1A 1PU

0 9 8 7 6 5 4 3 2 1

ACKNOWLEDGMENTS

Within the textile industry there is much information regarding design practices that is disseminated only by word of mouth, never having been collected and published so far as my assiduous search has discovered. Many friends, colleagues, and experts have kindly encouraged my belief that this material should be gathered comprehensively and accurately into a book; and it is with great joy and vast appreciation that I now try to thank them for so graciously and generously contributing their time and knowledge to its completion. Each can take credit for its success; none is responsible for its inadequacies; all have my profound gratitude.

I should like to thank in particular all the artists and companies who permitted me to use their work as illustrations. Bruno Pellegatta and the people at Cantoni and Jerry Newman and the people at Craftex Mills opened their doors to me, allowed me to photograph without restraint, and answered many questions. I am indeed grateful to those who, above and beyond what I could have possibly wished, kindly dug through archives and records to provide textiles and photographs that I needed. Martha de Llosa at American Fabrics Magazine, Ed Berkise and Lee Buchsbaum at American Silk Mills, Margot Dockrell at Brunschwig & Fils, Karen Allen at Gura Public Relations (for Lee Jofa), Gwen Ames and Diana Vila at Jay Yang Designs, Merle Lindby-Young at Knoll International, Pat Tunsky of Pat Tunsky, Inc., Linda Cuono at Ratti, Mendy Derketsch at Weave Corporation—all went well out of their way to help this project. Almuth Palinkas and Pam Turczyn made substantial contributions. Professor Alan Donaldson of North Carolina State University, Nancy Durrence, Shelly Gurton, Wendy Klein, and Sandy Rush provided guidance, encouragement, and information. Charles Blair of Blair Graphics and Michael Gorelick graciously contributed time, energy, and acumen.

Aimee Klitman at Andrews/Nelson/Whitehead and Arthur Steig at Steig Products helped immensely in clarifying matters for the materials chapter.

I should also like to thank Dr. Alice Zriebec of the Metropolitan Museum of Art and Professor Glen Kaufman of the

University of Georgia, who answered questions concerning historical accuracy.

I should mention in particular Michael D. Pitts for many of the line drawings throughout the text and for all photography that is not otherwise credited. Additionally, I thank Lynne Shapiro, Adelle Yates, and David Yates for proofreading the manuscript. My editor, Susan Gies, could not have been more supportive and helpful at all stages.

I am especially grateful for the enthusiastic encouragement I have received from Glen Kaufman, who critiqued and helped from my first thought of the book to its final draft. Finally, I have enjoyed continual encouragement and assistance from Sheila Hicks, Professor Neal Myers of the University of Hawaii, Peggy and Michael Pitts, Mr. and Mrs. Paul Yates, and, most of all, from Benjamin Weisgal.

ACKNOWLEDGMENTS FOR THE REVISED EDITION

In the time that has passed since I completed this book in its first edition, I have had the opportunity to collaborate with numerous talented textile designers. These admired colleagues inspire me to keep this text complete and current. Adrienne Concra, Margaret Dunford, Glen Kaufman, and Pam Turczyn were particularly generous in sharing their time and spirit. Ray Wenzel's high standards for our discipline and his ability to articulate its many facets were especially important.

Deborah Blum and Susan Slover simply never stop doing one exemplary piece of work after another, and encourage their friends to do the same. Nancy Green, surely the most steadfast of editors, receives my thanks not only for her support of my own work, but for her unending quest to reach readers who love fabric.

And I shall try again, but still I can never adequately thank my family: my son Bryan Weisgal, his grandparents, and especially my husband, Benjamin Weisgal.

CONTENTS

INTRODUCTION

This text was developed to inform artists with a strong background in basic design and color principles of a market for their creative work—the textile industry. University and college textile design courses usually emphasize methods of hand production and hand-decoration of fabric, yet in the United States alone billions of yards of cloth are commercially produced each year. Inventive approaches to the design of these textiles are always in demand.

With an overview of the textile industry and a thorough explanation of the designer's role, the text encourages adaptation of any design expertise into the processes, techniques, and formats characteristic of this industry.

This book is a compilation of information obtained from many designers. Because each designer may work for several years within only one segment of the market, this comprehensive view of studio practices throughout the industry should be meaningful even to practicing professionals.

A textile designer's job is multifaceted, requiring thorough understanding of the customer for whom the product is intended, knowledge of related and competing products and any sphere that influences the design world, and mastery of technical considerations of fabric production. Perhaps most importantly, a designer must be able at the appropriate time to present new ideas so that the intended market can understand and use them.

The backbone of the designer's career is his work in the studio. The development and completion of artwork on paper is the base from which the aesthetic aspects of fabric are produced. Consequently, practical studio methods not only make a designer more effective but also save time and money. Ideas for techniques, materials, and references encourage new interpretations and experimentation.

This book details a highly enjoyable career among enthusiastic professionals throughout an exciting industry.

TEXTILES

The Textile Industry

1

Soon after Samuel Slater had secretly brought over precious designs of textile machinery from England in the late eighteenth century, Eli Whitney invented the cotton gin. Thus began the mechanization and industrialization of the American textile industry. In the first few years of the nineteenth century in Lyon, France, Joseph J. M. Jacquard invented a loom, still in use today and now called by his name, in which the woven pattern is indicated by a set of punched cards and mechanically controlled, allowing elaborate and intricate patterns to be woven with much less manpower. A few years later, the first practical American power loom was built. Textile mills—where all operations, from the opening of the cotton bales to the finishing of the woven cloth, were mechanized and under one roof—came into existence. By 1860 more people were employed in textile mills than in any other American industry.

Today, although the advent of man-made fibers has allowed new applications for textile products and many more technological advances have been made, the processes of textile manufacture are still very much the same as they have always been (figures 1-2, 1-3). Cloth, one of man's basic needs, must be woven or knitted from yarn that is spun from fiber. In contemporary industry these processes are executed by diverse companies. Some textile organizations today own many huge, modern manufacturing plants using efficient and sophisticated machinery, while others have only a few employees and may not manufacture at all. Some American mills that have made very few changes in the past fifty years continue to manufacture fabric. Textiles are produced in almost every country, in some cases for that country's exclusive consumption but in most cases for export around the world. Some mills abroad are more technologically advanced than American mills, while in many countries fabric is handwoven on simple looms as it was centuries ago.

The industry is large and diverse. Its advances, as well as its resistance to change in the U.S. and abroad, make the American textile market what it is today.

The companies that constitute the American textile-related industries can be categorized in several ways.

First, these companies can be grouped by the organization's

Figure 1-1
Warping frame. A yarn from each cone is wound onto a beam to form the warp of a fabric.

products and the way in which these products are manufactured or processed.

Fabric is made from yarn, which is, in turn, made from either natural or man-made fiber. The natural fibers cotton and linen are produced by plants; wool and silk are produced by animals. Man-made fibers are synthetically made by chemical processes. Nylon, polyester, and acetate are examples; and these fibers are produced by large chemical companies, such as E. I. duPont de Nemours & Company, Hoechst-Celanese, Eastman, and Monsanto. These various companies produce no fabric but may specialize in the production of certain types of fiber, which they sell to fabric or yarn manufacturers in the raw fiber state or already processed into yarn.

Yarn producers buy natural or man-made fibers and spin them into yarns of different sizes and characters, which fabric manufacturers then weave or knit to produce a fabric.

Companies that own the necessary equipment and use it to produce fabric are called mills. Mills do not produce fiber but often spin their own yarn, which is woven or knitted in an undyed state to produce a fabric. This colorless fabric, before

Figure 1-2
Ming, printed cotton. (© *Jay Yang Designs Ltd.*)

being further processed, is termed *griege* (or gray) goods. Color is next added to these griege, or unfinished, goods by printing or dyeing (called piece-dyeing). Fabrics may instead be constructed of already dyed yarns; thus, once woven or knitted the *yarn-dyed* cloth is already colored and will not usually be dyed or printed.

Finishing—the final process before the textile is used—removes excess dye, sets the color, and also fluffs the yarns that make up the fabric to complete the structural aspect of the fabric. When desired, special finishing processes may be used to soften or stiffen the *hand* (the way the fabric feels when touched), make the fabric stain resistant, or add a sheen to the fabric.

Many large mills perform all of these processes; but small print plants, dye plants, and finishers may perform one of these functions, usually on a commission basis.

Because mills function on more than one of these manufacturing levels—that is, they produce yarn, griege goods, and finished fabric—these mills are called vertical, or vertically integrated operations. Most vertical mills (such as Burlington,

5

J. P. Stevens, Milliken, and Dan River) sell fabric directly to manufacturers of clothes and furniture. They may also sell fabric to *converters*. A converter buys griege goods and "converts" it into finished fabric according to his own specifications by having it dyed, printed, and finished on commission by a third company. Whereas a mill owns specific equipment, which must be kept in operation to maintain profitability, the fact that a converter does not own any equipment allows broad flexibility in the types of fabric he can pioneer. Although he may be under contract with his suppliers, if a converter has an idea for a new fabric that he believes he can sell, he has the option of finding a new resource to produce the new item without compromising his existing converting operation. A mill, on the other hand, has all operations under its own roof, thereby maintaining more complete control.

Fabrics are produced by the *piece,* which usually ranges from 30 to 80 yards of fabric depending on the weight and difficulty in production of the goods. Piece lengths of 60 to 70 yards are most common. Mills and converters sell by the piece to manufacturers of clothing and furniture as well as to large retail stores, which sell to consumers for home sewing purposes. In the area of fabrics for interiors, both mills and converters sell to *jobbers*. By definition, a jobber buys a product in quantity and without changing the product sells it in smaller quantities to a new customer. A jobber may be a middleman who buys overruns and close-out lots from manufacturers and sells them to retail stores or smaller manufacturers. In textiles, the term *jobber* usually refers to a company that buys upholstery or drapery fabric by the piece from mills and converters and sells *cut yardage* (less than a piece) to the end consumer through architects and interior designers. Most of the well-known fabric houses that sell expensive fabric to interior designers are called jobbers.

A company may fall into more than one of these classifications. For example, a domestic mill produces fabrics, but may convert a fabric, from a foreign mill, that is complementary to its domestically produced line, but which is uneconomical for the mill to manufacture. A jobber may buy fabric from converters but go directly to mills to convert other types of goods. Some jobbers even own small mills that produce a portion of their lines. A textile company is usually labeled by the function for which it is primarily known to its suppliers and customers.

Textile companies are likewise known for the end use of their fabrics. Mills may produce fabrics for various segments

6

of the market, but most converters develop fabrics exclusively for one end use.

The apparel industry is a large consumer of textile products. Therefore, a textile company may orient its products toward manufacturers of women's dresses, women's sportswear; men's wear; outerwear (coats), or neckties. Children's wear; active wear; dance wear; hosiery, swimsuits, gloves, handbags, scarves, hats, umbrellas, and uniforms are other apparel markets.

Domestics include sheets, towels, bedspreads, shower curtains, "table top" (placemats, tablecloths, and napkins), and decorative pillows. Sheets and towels are usually produced by vertical mills, which weave, print, finish, sew, and sell the consumer-ready product directly to retail stores. Other domestic products are developed by converters as well as by mills.

Fabrics for upholstery, drapery, wall covering, and floor covering fall into two categories: those for home use (called the *decorative, residential,* or *home furnishings* area), and those for commercial use, such as offices, hotels, or hospital interiors (called the *contract* area). A mill, converter, or jobber may concentrate on any combination of these areas—for example, decorative and contract drapery or contract upholstery and drapery.

Textiles are also produced for industrial uses. These fabrics are developed to meet specific requirements, and aesthetic value is of little importance for such uses as automobile tires, parachutes, conveyor belts, space suits, typewriter ribbons, and industrial hoses. Textiles are also used in automobile and airplane interiors, and in some luggage and shoes, and for these uses aesthetics are as important as specific technical requirements.

Additionally, all fabric sources are commonly categorized by the price range of their product. Companies selling expensive fabric are called high end, upper end, or, in the field of interior textiles, uptown (because these companies are uptown in New York City).

The largest quantity of all fabrics is sold in middle price ranges; therefore companies producing such fabrics are called volume, or middle, market. Lower end, or downtown, fabric houses sell even less expensive goods.

Thus, any textile company will be described using various labels. A "volume drapery converter" and a "mill that produces high-end dress fabrics" conjure up two very different pictures: producers of textile products that operate differently and sell to different markets in terms of both end use and price point.

Textile organizations in other countries can be categorized similarly. The large European mills tend to be very modern

Figure 1-3
Loom with Jacquard head.

and sophisticated but smaller than the largest American mills. On the other hand, after perhaps centuries, craftsmen in small European operations continue to produce items peculiar to their specific area. These products are handled through European converters or are directly imported by American converters, jobbers, or apparel manufacturers. Similar small operations exist in other countries and export their goods; such individual craftsmen rarely produce on a commercial scale in the United States. Jobbers are less common in Europe; expensive home-furnishing fabrics are usually sold directly from converters through retail stores to the end consumer.

Large volumes of textiles are now produced and exported to the United States by Far Eastern countries. These goods are largely manufactured by modern vertically integrated mills and sold to the United States by large trading countries.

Countries ranging from India to New Zealand and Brazil manufacture and export textiles to the United States. These may be large- or small-volume operations and usually sell to converters, jobbers, and apparel manufacturers through an American sales agent.

The Role of Textile Designers

Although aesthetics are obviously more important in some textiles than in others, visual appeal is a factor in any commercial product. In industrial textiles, aesthetics are less important than other factors in the development of the product, but even a company that produces industrial sewing thread must know which colors of thread to produce and how to display the product for the best appeal to its customers. However, in most areas of the textile market, the appearance and the hand of the fabric are two of its most important aspects. Textiles are largely used to decorate or embellish, whether a person, a sofa, or a window. The role of the textile designer in industry is to guide the development of desirable appearance and hand in fabrics.

The manufacturing facilities of most American textile mills are located in small towns in the North and Southeast but are headquartered in New York City, where the design staffs are usually located. The size of the mill's design staff depends on the company's size, but it usually consists of one design director, a stylist for each division, and several artists.

If a company is large enough to have more than one stylist, the design director has responsibility for all areas and phases of the company's artistic direction. All artists and designers within the company report to him, and he probably reports to the president of the company.

A stylist handles the development of the fabric company's *line,* which is the group of fabrics designed, developed, and edited to be shown and sold to the market each season. The stylist initiates the line, organizes and directs the artists in the development and coloration of intended designs, coordinates with manufacturing personnel to have the samples produced that will be shown to customers, and then edits and finalizes the group of designs to be shown for the season. A stylist may or may not do the actual artwork on paper but is responsible for knowing what product the company should be making at a particular time and must make the product line a reality at the proper time.

The artists who work in the studio of a textile mill do the actual artwork on paper in preparation for production of textiles. These artists may be designers who do complete textile designs, repeat artists who put designs into the size and repeat appropriate for the specific company's needs, or colorists who do the actual renderings and try different color looks for every design.

A mill stylist is a designer who works at the textile manufacturing plant to make certain that the first time a new design goes into production it is executed as the head stylist instructed. Very few mills have full-time mill stylists. Usually on a rotating basis, the stylist or the studio staff will travel to the mill when it is time for the first sample run (called a strike-off) to be produced.

These various jobs for textile designers may overlap; or one person may do more than one of these jobs, depending on the talents of the designer and the company's organizational structure.

Design departments of converters are analogous to those of mills but are usually smaller, since most converters are smaller than most mills.

Textile designers may also work for independent studios, which produce and sell designs on paper to mills and converters. A designer is usually not a true employee of a studio but rather produces designs on a free-lance basis for which the studio receives a commission when the designs are sold.

Textile designers often work on a free-lance basis without working through a studio. A designer may show artwork to stylists from mills and converters who then buy them and have their companies produce the designs. A stylist may also contact a free-lance designer to develop a design according to

9

the stylist's specifications or even to do mill styling. A group of free-lance designers may also be represented by an agent who sells the designs to mills and converters on commission. Free-lance designers, producing on speculation, and selling in the U.S. and Europe through studios or agents, seem more prevalently European than American.

Because jobbers do not produce fabric, design directors for these companies usually choose the group of fabrics that the jobber should carry. In small jobbers, this selection is often made by the president or owner of the company. Design directors may be called fabric coordinators or directors of fabric merchandising. Similar positions exist with some clothing manufacturers, although in these companies fabrics usually are chosen by the clothing designer. Some retail stores also employ fashion coordinators who organize presentations to show their buyers what fabrics the store management wants to emphasize.

Many textile designers work in such related areas as wrapping paper, greeting cards, dinnerware, tile, and giftware. These are not textile products, but the design considerations in these areas are comparable to surface decoration of fabric.

Timing in the Textile Industry

Every segment of textile-related industries plans and produces products well ahead of retail selling seasons. Before fall clothing appears in stores at the time that consumers want to buy such garments, the clothes must be designed, shown to stores, sold, and produced. Before the clothing can be designed, fabrics must be designed, shown to clothing manufacturers, sold, and produced (figure 1–4). Before that, new yarns and fibers must be developed. The scheduling and amount of time necessary for all of these steps depends on the amount of change that is occurring in the product, the volume being produced, and the efficiency of the companies involved. At a minimum, however, textiles are designed a year and a half ahead of the retail selling season. (Design of fabric for next fall's clothing must begin in spring of this year.) Major changes, such as development of a completely new type of fabric for a mill, will take even longer to effect.

Textiles for apparel are shown to clothing manufacturers at two main selling seasons: spring, in April and May, a year ahead of the retail spring for which the fabric is intended, and fall, in October and November. Holiday and resort are smaller seasons that follow fall; summer follows spring, and fall is sometimes broken into fall I and fall II.

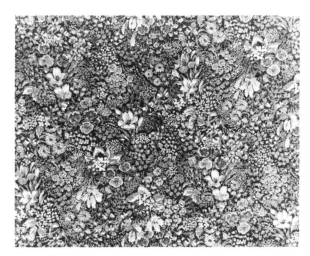

Figure 1-4
Floral, printed cotton velveteen. (© *Cantoni Satilai*)

Furniture manufacturers look at new fabrics in June and December, again several months before the furniture appears in stores. Jobbers look at new upholstery and drapery fabrics in April and October, although jobbers tend to be less restricted to specific selling seasons and may add to their lines all year round.

In every segment of the market, the large-volume manufacturers work even farther ahead; and the higher-end companies work very close to the selling season. This is partly because the leading designers want more time to develop new ideas, but also because their smaller operations do not require the long lead time (that is, preparation time) necessary for large-volume production runs.

The Designer's Projections of Market Trends

In the manufacture of fabrics, as in any other discipline of design, maintaining and even surpassing high aesthetic standards are a designer's primary goals. Proportion, balance, and texture are attained through expert draftsmanship. Tasteful and innovative use of color is an innate ability developed through study and practice. However, in any commercial enterprise, formulating a general assignment for design of product lines must also involve accounting for both the suitability of the design for the end product and maximizing use of available materials and manufacturing capabilities. For fabric designers, the technical facets of this problem should be studied in textile science courses and through several excellent texts. Without an understanding of how visual ideas can be used in manufacturing processes and an ability to articu-

11

late these ideas to technical personnel, a designer's innovative ideas may be wasted.

In industry, textile companies look to designers or stylists to see, understand, and capture current and future trends in color and pattern. A designer must guide a company to use its capabilities fully in producing new, different, and timely fabrics.

In addition to keeping abreast of technical information and keeping artistic skills well honed, a designer/stylist must be able to anticipate future trends and coordinate the release of new fabrics at the time for best marketability.

How are future trends anticipated? In part through awareness of past and present work in the field. Historically, certain trends are cyclical, largely because consumers tire of one look and want a change after some time has passed. If black is prevalent in clothing one year, it will probably appear in home furnishings the next year, and color will then seem a refreshing change in clothing. But will black be followed by bright colors, or by brown with colored accents, or by pastels? Through intuitive ability and research, a designer must commit to the coming trends well ahead of the time that clothes appear in stores.

Historical fabrics may be studied from books and old magazines and are a limitless source of inspiration and information. Local museums and historical societies may have textile or costume collections (figure 1–5). Some textile companies maintain extensive archives that are almost museums in themselves.

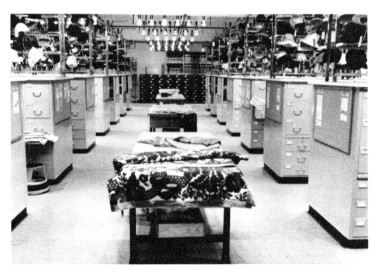

Figure 1–5
As members of the Edward C. Blum Design Laboratory at the Fashion Institute of Technology in New York City, designers may research collections and utilize the world's largest collection of textile swatches and costumes. (*Photograph courtesy of the Design Laboratory*)

Exhibitions of fabrics in major museums are wonderful for study and may also effect a trend by drawing attention to a particular era of fabrics. The "blockbuster" exhibitions of the seventies and eighties have been replaced by small shows and greater cultural awareness, ensuring that influences come from a diverse array of sources.

To keep abreast of current trends, most designers in the industry read trade periodicals and reports from forecasters, and travel to the major trade shows in the United States and Europe. Manufacturers or designers of fabric, clothes, or furniture display their newest group of products—called a *line, collection,* or *range*—to buyers, individually, in their showrooms. In each segment of the industry the lines are ready to show at the start of a particular selling season. Often companies in one area of the market assemble together at the beginning of the selling season. Buyers come to these *trade shows* during *market week* to place orders or to make plans to place orders soon thereafter. These shows also allow everyone a chance to see what is newest in the market. Trade shows are often abused by competitors looking for items that can be readily *knocked off* (that is, copied). When these markets are used as intended, they serve as a healthy forum for all to observe new designs that are already selling. These exhibitions are open only to members of the trade and the press but are also thoroughly reported in current periodicals.

Women's Wear Daily (WWD) is probably the most widely read trade periodical. Because trends in women's apparel affect all segments of the market, *WWD* is read regularly even by home furnishings and men's wear executives. *Vogue* and *Bazaar* magazines, both of which are published in American, French, and Italian editions that cover their respective markets, are at the forefront of fashion reporting. Other magazines published abroad (*Linea Italiana, Gap Italia*) and domestically (*Glamour, Mademoiselle*) are excellent sources of information.

In men's wear, Daily News Record (DNR) is the equivalent of Women's Wear Daily, and DNR also covers technical news of the textile industry. Vogue, Linea, and other periodicals publish a men's wear edition. Gentlemen's Quarterly is a popular American source.

In home furnishing/contract interiors, most designers read *Architectural Digest, Elle Decor, Interiors, Interior Design,* and *Metropolitan Home.* European periodicals such as *World of Interiors, Elle Decoration, Casa Vogue,* and *Decoration Internationale* are popular. *Home Furnishings Daily* is the weekly that covers furniture, textiles, giftware, and electronics.

13

No designer has time to read all of these periodicals, but most regularly read a few that they consider most valuable and frequently glance through others. Periodicals are an easily accessible means of viewing developments within the entire industry.

In addition to periodicals, various market reports are excellent vehicles for study of current developments in the industry, and they may be available in some libraries or schools. These various color and trend forecasting services in the United States and Europe obtain their information in different ways and therefore offer various points of view.

Some forecasters do essentially the same research that designers and textile executives do; but because market research is the main profession of forecasters, they may see more than one designer could. A forecaster also sees textile manufacturers' developmental fabrics a few weeks before the finished line is shown to customers. The forecaster is thereby able to draw conclusions about the overall marketplace before the start of the selling season. A designer, on the other hand, would be able to see his competitor's line only after it is already on the market. A report projecting the coming season well in advance (geared for a specific segment of the market such as women's wear, men's wear, or interiors) may consist of a color palette of solids, good color combinations from the palette, and information on important types of textiles (figure 1–6). Fore-

Figure 1–6
"Colors" is the product presented three times a year to clients of Color Projections, Inc./Pat Tunsky, Inc., that shows new colors and color combinations for the upcoming season.

casters also advise their clients (the designers who subscribe to their reports) individually.

Most color forecasters also forecast "trends" in clothing silhouette, construction, and types of fabric that will be suitable. An individual forecaster may emphasize one of these areas over another.

Promostyl, founded in the 1960s, is the oldest forecasting service of this type. Pat Tunsky, Inc., established in 1972, forecasts color, fabric, design, and interior color trends geared to American manufacturers. The Color Box and Huepoint provide color information. Trend Union is the most important French source. Originally a men's wear trend service, Design Intelligence, based in London, is still very strong in men's wear. *Interior View, View on Color,* and *Textile View* are periodicals that offer such information to a broad audience.

The Color Association of the United States (CAUS) has been issuing color projections (figure 1–7) for women's wear since the 1920s and for interiors since the 1950s. Projections are based on the palette selection made by a panel of successful designers and marketing executives selected by CAUS from industry. This provides a different type of information from that provided by the aforementioned services. Rather than showing information obtained specifically to be forecast, the CAUS palette shows the thinking of certain "leaders" within a segment of the industry.

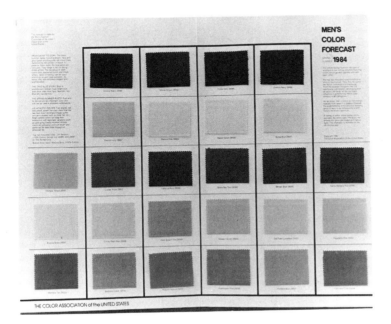

Figure 1–7
The Color Association of the United States shows its forecasting board's results on cards that are distributed to its members semi-annually.

The International Color Authority (ICA), based in Europe, operates similarly to CAUS.

Other groups, especially in Europe, are similar in operation to the original concept of CAUS. Representatives from a group of mills, usually in a particular country, will develop and promote a palette for their products. The Société de la Fédération de la Soierie in France is such an organization, as is Comitato Italiano del Colore in Italy. Likewise, organizations such as Cotton, Inc., and the Wool Bureau, which are supported by producers of the appropriate fiber to promote its use, develop color forecasts.

The Color Marketing Group allows interaction and discussion among designers from all disciplines at large national meetings. Members discuss in small groups and then vote on a palette which is geared to a particular segment of the market.

No service provides an absolute answer, but information and interaction among design professionals help to inform everyone. Additionally, forecasters not only observe and predict but effect trends. For all of these reasons designers must be aware of these reports, which are a considerable force in the business of design.

Some magazines have departments that cover specifically the fabric market. Editors from these magazines report seasonally their findings in the market and from the major shows. Presentations are made by *Vogue, Mademoiselle, Bazaar,* and others to designers, buyers, and other fashion executives. Large buying offices for major stores also make similar presentations. Likewise, the major fiber companies (Eastman, Hoechst-Celanese, Monsanto, etc.) forecast colors and make seasonal market reports to their customers. Fiber companies were among the first to make these reports; but because they produce synthetic fibers and sell mostly to large mills and manufacturers, their reports are geared to the volume (middle) market.

Designers also study direct market response to their specific product. Sales reports within an individual textile firm are broken down by customer, type of fabric, and color so that the company's personnel may draw conclusions about rising or dying trends. By working directly with customers (for example, manufacturers of clothing or furniture, and distributors of fabric who sell to architects or interior designers), textile designers learn quickly what items and ideas are acceptable and at what price. The relationship works in two ways: a designer's job is not only to respond to customers' demands but also to cultivate taste within the public. When a designer receives negative reaction to a product that he believes indi-

idea but tries to find a way to show the idea in another way that will be better accepted. Textile businesses involve a lot of middlemen; at each level the customer (who is sometimes a designer himself) must choose the newly designed fabric before it reaches the retail customer. If the product is not considered to be salable, the public will never see the design.

In addition to occurrences within the textile-related industries, any current trend will affect design. A popular movie with costumes from the 1920s will influence the next season's fashions. For example, a major museum show, a Broadway play, or a new First Lady with her own sense of style all whet the desires of the consumer and therefore the textile industry. The availability or shortage of certain materials affects design; if cotton is in short supply, other fibers will be developed and styled into fabrics to simulate cotton fabrics. New developments in lighting will affect trends in interiors and therefore the kinds of furniture and fabrics that will be desirable.

Probably one of the best sources of inspiration is from

Figure 1–8
La Scala (lower left) and *Tosca* (right), Jacquard wovens. (© *Arc-Com Fabrics, photograph courtesy Arc-Com*)

images in other art forms that can be applied to textiles (figures 1–9, 1–10, 1–11). Images, techniques, and color combinations in art history, graphic design, or illustration inspire fabric designers. An Italian fresco could make a beautiful fabric. Or the way that a certain color works with another in a Cezanne painting could inspire a color line of fabric.

As a designer studies and observes, reference files of interesting subject matter, technique, and color are compiled. This file may contain photographs of color looks, fashions, flowers and plants, or scraps of fabric and paint chips that can serve as color references. It is even more important that designers keep notebooks and sketch books of interesting images (figure

18

Figure 1–10
Geometric design, reminiscent of op art patterns. Gouache on waxed *masa* paper. (© *N.J. Cohen*)

1–12). Quick, small sketches from daily life can serve as an excellent reference which can be further developed.

A good designer must keep up with any facet of life which can affect the design world but, more importantly, must never be confined to work that has been done before or is being done currently. The textile industry, like any business, likes to continue with products that are known to be salable. However, a new idea, expressed in a new way and well presented, will boost sales. In essence, textile design is the marketing of these new ideas.

Figure 1–11
Waves and Stripes, watercolor on paper, achieves an art deco feeling in motif and technique. (© *1980 Almuth Palinkas, photograph courtesy the artist*)

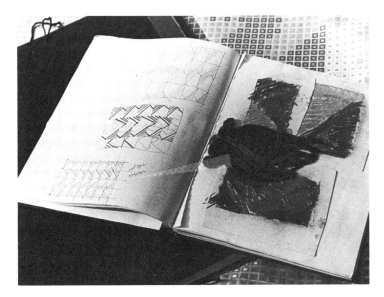

Figure 1–12
A designer's sketchbook shows color studies, yarn swatches, and rough drawings of geometric motifs.

2 Materials

Most printed textiles and some woven textiles are designed as drawings or paintings, usually on paper. This artwork is reproduced through the actual fabrication of the textile in the case of weaving, or by superimposition of the pattern onto an already existing fabric by using printing processes.

Any medium can be used in the artwork, but materials with which designers can achieve facsimiles of particular effects in manufactured fabrics allow design problems to be more accurately resolved in the studio before the pattern is put into production. More expense and headaches are avoided by throwing away a painted piece of paper and starting again than doing likewise with many yards of fabric.

It is easy to see that lightweight, translucent papers readily absorbing watercolor paint correspond to lightweight, translucent apparel or drapery fabrics that are printed so that the dye is accepted by the fibers. A sturdy paper that holds paint on its surface is more similar to a smooth upholstery fabric heavy enough to prevent complete penetration of the dye. Special effects, such as wax-resist *batik* dying methods, can be simulated on paper using certain materials and techniques. In industry, specific painting techniques have become standard representations of corresponding fabric printing methods. Textile designers constantly search for materials that allow them to replicate specific manufactured fabrics. Conversely, with current printing technology it is possible to interpret on fabric almost any rendering on paper; thus, a designer's use of materials not only simulates standard textile effects but pushes new methods of fabric decoration into popular use. Innovative and interesting work on paper will warrant development or adaptation of technology to produce more interesting textiles.

Varied materials of good quality are therefore of critical importance. The artist's repertoire should not be limited by lack of versatile tools or by imprecise, poorly made equipment. If a designer is unable to convey an idea explicitly on paper, the fabric will certainly never match the designer's expectations.

Although initially expensive, the investment in the best materials will pay off quickly because this quality is directly reflected in artwork. It cannot be overemphasized that the best craftsmanship cannot compensate for shoddy raw materials.

Artist's materials change, and new products are constantly available. Catalogues from art supply sources are full of useful information about materials and are usually available at no cost.

Paints

The artwork on paper which will be reproduced on fabric by printing or weaving is usually created in one of two media: gouache and concentrated bottled watercolor.

Gouache (figure 2–1) is essentially watercolor with white pigment added for opacity. Gum arabic is the binder, as in watercolor, although some gouache colors also contain a plastic emulsion and so are waterproof when dry. Colors are made from different pigments that have varying physical properties, including opacity: "thalo" (short for phthalocyanine) blue and alizarin crimson are translucent; the cadmiums and burnt and raw umber are more opaque. The quality and large selection of colors available from Winsor Newton (labeled "Designer's Gouache") are preferred by most designers. Pelikan is also good, although more fillers are added to its colors to give more consistent opacity and viscosity between varying pigments. Grumbacher's gouache is in less common use among designers. Turner's gouache, from Japan, is available in larger tubes than Winsor Newton but in a smaller color range. Although the colors are brilliant, they seem to contain a lot of binder. Linel, from Germany, is available in a very large color range.

Poster and tempera colors, such as Rich Art brand, are packaged in jars (figure 2–2). Unlike gouache, they are made with eggs as a binder, but because they are opaque and water based, they can be compatibly mixed with gouache colors. With less pigment and more filler than gouache, poster and tempera are generally not suitable for professional use. The exception is white: the difference in appearance between qualities of white paint is negligible; and because such large quantities of white paint are required, the less expensive brand is acceptable to most designers. Poster color is also excellent for rough sketches as preparation before the final rendering. It is common to keep different colors of poster color in individual squeeze bottles (from the drug store) for easy access.

As its name implies, bleed-proof white paint, made by both Luma and Dr. Ph. Martin's, will cover very dark or intense colors even if painted very thinly (figure 2–3).

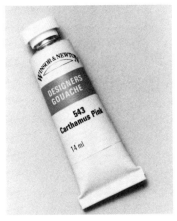

Figure 2–1
Designer's gouache. (*Photograph courtesy Winsor & Newton*)

Figure 2–2
Poster color. (*Photograph courtesy Rich Art*)

Figure 2-3
Bleed-proof white. (*Photograph courtesy Luma*)

A tiny bit of white gouache, water, and gum arabic added to a particular watercolor shade will approximate a corresponding gouache color. Consistency of paint surface, which is important in the final artwork, is difficult to maintain with this mixture; but for rough sketching, mixing a striking shade, or even completing a project under deadline after running out of a crucial gouache shade, this recipe can be useful.

Gouache has a relatively short shelf life because it can dry out in the tube; therefore, it should be bought as needed and be carefully stored with a tightly closed cap after use. By placing a little bit of lubricating jelly or glycerine on the threads of the tube, the caps will be less likely to dry shut. Metal caps are also less likely than plastic ones to stick to the top of the tube.

Additions will be constantly made to the basic palette, but a designer must begin with a wide variety of colors because mixing more than three colors together to obtain a desired shade greatly increases the muddiness of the mixture. A starting palette that covers the spectrum could include lemon yellow, which is clear, and yellow ochre, which is an earth-toned pigment; two or three greens, such as permanent green (medium or light) or cypress green; a straight blue, such as cobalt or cerulean; a redder blue like ultramarine, and a turquoise; a range of reds, including alizarin crimson, bengal rose, rose carthame, and havannah lake; a rich brown, like burnt or raw umber; jet black, which is cool, and lamp black, which is warm.

A unique characteristic of rose carthame must be remarked. It is a very luminous, rich, transparent pink; but it is also extremely strong. One drop of carthamus pink will alter a pot of paint; and carthamus pink, once painted, cannot be painted over even with bleed-proof paint.

Gouache, like any opaque medium, achieves whites and tints by use of white pigment, which combined with the binder used yields a matte, chalky quality. With some degree of expertise, an artist can produce an absolutely flat surface in this medium. By contrast, any type of watercolor has a luminous surface. For the whites and pale tones it utilizes the shine of the paper brilliantly showing through the translucent paint, which is diluted with water to produce variety of color value. This glaze system of pigmentation is as appropriate for certain effects as the opaque method is for other results.

True watercolors are made from insoluble pigments dispersed into a binder, gum arabic, which holds the pigment particles together and protects them from outside influences. Designer's *concentrated watercolors* are actually aniline (figure 2–4). These soluble pigments are mostly synthetic substances that are dissolved in a solution and bond physically with the surface onto which they are applied. Because the pigments are soluble and thus need no binder, the paints are more transparent and brilliant, and mix and brush more readily than true watercolors. Most of these soluble pigments, however, are *fugitive* colors; that is, the color fades quickly when the painting is exposed to light. Although the quality of draftsmanship and painterliness in a textile design should in no way be lower than that of any piece of art, the eventual aim is to transfer the work to a piece of fabric. The original artwork must endure considerable handling in the studio and during mill work; but the artwork is usually thought of more as a record of the textile, which should itself be the finished artwork.

Luma is by far the most common brand of concentrated watercolor used in textiles. Dr. Martin's is also good. Some designers feel that it is not so concentrated as Luma and for this reason is well suited for use with airbrush. Both brands come in small bottles with eyedropper tops for convenience. Luma's availability in larger bottles may be a major reason why it is the more prevalent brand. Luma is also available in a much larger range of colors. Kept tightly closed, bottle colors (or "dyes") will last indefinitely, allowing a designer to maintain a broad palette at all times. A beginning range includes a variety of browns such as antelope, saddle, and tobacco; amber, lemon, indian, and daffodil yellows; orange; tropic pink; flame red; rose tyrien; moss rose; cyclamen; persimmon; pansy; turquoise; aquamarine; ultramarine and slate blue; moss and calypso greens; sepia; and black.

Figure 2–4
Bottled watercolor. (*Photograph courtesy Luma*)

Papers

Almost every textile design is executed on a paper surface, and an extremely wide range of papers is available. Certain techniques or desired results require specific papers, but it is largely up to the individual artist to determine which one will be most suitable to achieve the desired result. The paper, combined with the technique used, should give the most accurate rendering possible of how the actual fabric will look. For example, if the fabric to be printed is heavy and off-white, it would not make sense to paint the design on a white, translucent ground. Gouache can be used on any of the papers listed; because dye is translucent, it is unsuitable for dark papers.

Watercolor paper is ideal for dye, and comes in different

23

textures: hot pressed (HP), cold pressed (CP), not pressed (NP), and rough. Cold pressed and not pressed are a medium texture, good for line and wash, and easiest for beginners to handle. The surface of hot pressed is shiny and may be too harsh for washes but is good for fine line and opaque media. Rough, as is implied, has a definite toothy surface and can produce unusual effects with washes and with dry brush techniques. Good drawing papers are available in these surfaces also and are excellent design options. Some papers come only in white, some in white or buff. Handmade papers of high linen rag content will deteriorate very little if properly stored and cared for, and as they are usually sized properly, absorbency of the paper is regulated. (Some papers are sized only on the side on which the watermark is legible.) The expense of such paper may or may not be warranted, depending on the degree of permanence that the artist desires. Paper weights measure the weight of a ream, which is usually considered to be five hundred sheets of paper. Seventy-two-pound paper is relatively lightweight and needs to be stretched before it can be used with wet media; 90–140-pound paper is probably most desirable, although some excellent papers are available in weights up to 400 pounds. Good watercolor paper can be reused by soaking the entire painted sheet in a tub of clean, warm water. The painting will come off with a bit of gentle agitation, and the clean paper should then be hung to dry. Recommended brands of watercolor and drawing paper include Arches, Rives, Fabriano, and Strathmore. Some other popular brands are Bienfang, Grumbacher, and Morilla.

Bristol board (sometimes called "stretch paper") is unsuitable for use with dyes and is less desirable for use with gouache than watercolor paper; but because it is relatively inexpensive, it is in common use in industry, especially for painting yarn-dyed plaids and in the decorative area. "Kid" is the most suitable finish, and Bristol is available in different-size sheets and in large rolls. Bristol board, Beckett cover, and Starwhite cover are all available in large sizes and are popular as mounting boards for designs.

"Rice" paper, produced mostly in Japan, is actually a misnomer. Made primarily of *kozo* and/or *mitsumata,* which are indigenous Japanese shrubs with extremely long fibers, these papers are strong but likewise soft and supple. They are extremely absorbent, providing an excellent surface for dye and for many special painting techniques. Painting in dye on Japanese papers produces a strikingly accurate rendering of printed silk or polyester dress fabrics.

Of the various sorts of Japanese papers available, the one

most commonly used by textile designers is called *masa*. The rough side of *masa* paper is the correct side. Papers of similar appearance to *masa* but of varying weights include *hosho, goyu, iyo* glazed, *kochi,* and *torinoko,* which are Japanese papers, and *troya,* which is an American-made paper. Unlike *masa,* these papers are all suitable paint surfaces on either side. Japanese papers also come in off-white colors (*bitchu torinoko, gampi torinoko,* Japanese etching, *kitakata, okawara, tosa hanga*) and in silky textures with visible fibers imbedded into both sides (*inomachi, kinwashi, natsume, ogura, tairei,* and *unryu*). Special papers include *chiri* and fantasy, which have plant parts imbedded, and lace papers. *Moriki* and *unryu* are available in colors.

Figure 2–5
Wax Grip. (*Photograph courtesy Luma*)

Also available is waxed *masa,* impregnated with wax on both sides and resembling heavy tracing vellum but with a tooth on one side. Either side can be used, and the paper is a popular and excellent surface for dye and special painting techniques. A binder, called Wax Grip or Noncrawl, must be added to paint for it to adhere to the waxy surface (figure 2–5). A drop or two of liquid soap can be used instead, but it is probably best to test either substance to determine its suitability for a certain design. Any of these binders may change the paint color slightly, and soap will change it more than the other substances.

Rice paper sizes differ with each type but are approximately 20″ × 30″ *Masa* is available in large rolls. "Imperial" size (22″ × 30″) is the commonly available size of watercolor and drawing paper. Sheets of any paper can be spliced together for a larger design. In the decorative area, where large designs are more prevalent, certain papers are popular because of their large size. These include Bristol board, Beau Brilliant, Carousel, Sam Flax's 814 and 816 drawing papers, and Starwhite cover, all of which have different textures. A specific paper may be used extensively in one area because it is the exact size of the product for which the design is intended (for example, a bath towel or pillowcase).

Special surfaces, textures, and colors may be found in countless other papers. Oatmeal, tweedweave, and coquille are unusual surfaces; velour paper is fuzzy. Mylar (metallic), Flint (colors), and Fantasia Bristol (black or white) are luxuriously shiny. Pantone and Color-Aid are available in broad color ranges. Color-Aid paper is washable, allowing painted marks to be removed and changed during the final rendering. Any paper, from brown wrapping paper to butcher's paper, may be useful for a particular piece.

Designs may be painted in gouache on prepared acetate to

25

be superimposed over an already existing background. Changes can also be made on an acetate overlay, which is attached to a croquis, thus testing the change without disturbing the already painted surface. Because unprepared acetate is difficult to paint on even with Wax Grip or Noncrawl added, it is most often used to cover and protect finished artwork. A painting on any acetate will always be a little streaky.

Saral paper, like carbon paper but graphite backed, is available in sheets or small boxed rolls (like aluminum foil). It is used to transfer some layouts to the final ground paper.

Graph paper, or "point paper," can be used to help align elements in a layout or as a guideline for scaling motifs to a particular size. It is also used in designing weaves for Jacquard fabrics. Various scales of paper are available, with 4×4 spaces to an inch, 8×8, etc.

Last but not least, designers use endless quantities of tracing paper. Rolls of the least expensive sort are fine, but colorless tracing paper is preferred to the yellowish tinted type because the color can be distracting.

Although it is not usually necessary, more expensive tracing vellum is sturdier and may be worthwhile for detailed layouts that require more handling while in progress. Some vellums are very translucent, allowing ease in tracing a detailed document. Vellum may be used as a ground paper for designs and can be very convenient because its washable surface allows removal of gouache marks during the final painting.

Brushes

The designer's brushes (figure 2–6) are his most important tool, and no compromise or skimping should be considered in this area. Without the highest-quality sable brushes, detailed

Figure 2–6
Series 7 Kolinsky sable brushes. (*Photograph courtesy Winsor & Newton*)

work in gouache or watercolor is almost impossible, and inexpensive brushes do not last long. By buying a basic range of expensive brushes, taking care of them, and slowly adding to the collection, the artist will be rewarded for this investment with increased design capability that will show in the finished work.

Brush sizes are standardized internationally and range from sizes 000 to 14. Larger sizes are available but are especially uncommon in watercolor because it is a finer medium than oil. A designer's tools should include a good range of round points in various sizes and possibly one or two chisel points. The difference between a large or small brush is the amount of paint that it holds. All good brushes should make a point fine enough to render small details. The finest brushes are made of hair from the tail of the kolinsky (also called Siberian mink or red Tartar marten). Winsor Newton Series 7 are brushes of this quality; "pure red sables" are the next level below kolinsky sables.

A simple test for a new brush is to wet it, shake it dry, and then roll the point in the hand. The brush should make one full shape coming to a clear point, with no concavity between its point and its belly. Without this resiliency and sharpness the brush will never perform well.

It is a good idea to mark one good brush (possibly with a piece of masking tape) for use with white paint only. If no other color is ever used with this brush, it will always produce clear, white strokes.

A "French quill" is a special type of sable brush with a fine, long-lasting point available in a range of sizes. Because the point is long, the bristles are able to hold more paint.

Sparsely bristled, flat fan brushes can delicately manipulate wet surfaces, soften sharp contours, and make unique marks.

Additionally necessary are several mixing brushes with short, stiff bristles and one good-quality 2″ varnish or sign cutter's brush for painting flat grounds. It is just as important that these brushes be of good quality, since the bristles of inferior brushes break and fall out.

Brushes must be carefully cleaned and stored. Because gouache and dye are both water soluble, brushes should be rinsed in a water jar after each use while working. Allowing paint or ink to dry in the hair can damage a brush irreparably. The brush is kept soft and clean and then washed with soap and water after every work session. After a thorough rinsing, the bristles must be reshaped into a point. Brushes should never be moistened with the mouth because many chemicals

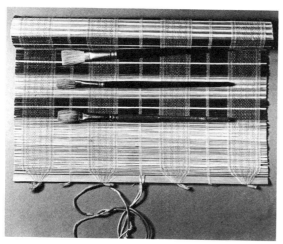

Figure 2-7
Brushes are laid flat and the *fudemaki* rolled and tied closed as convenient storage for brushes.

in paints are toxic and can cause various degrees of harm if ingested.

Brushes must be stored upright, with bristles up, or laid flat. For carrying, brushes may be carefully laid on a bamboo placemat (called a *fudemaki*) which can be rolled and then tied with a thread or rubber band (figure 2–7). If out of use for a length of time, brushes should be stored with moth balls or moth flakes.

A designer should mark brushes and all expensive tools with his name to avoid confusion among co-workers in a studio. This can be easily done with nail polish or by scratching into the wooden handle with a pushpin.

Pens and Inks

As with other materials, any pen that has a new or different capability is useful for the textile designer. With so many pens on the market today it would seem that a perfect one would exist. Not so; many of them are excellent, but for different uses.

Disposable pens, like felt- and fiber-tip markers, in a range that varies in color, value, and type of tip (thick, thin, flat, or pointed), are excellent for sketches and for certain effects (figure 2–8). A marker produces different hues and values with varying papers. Pantone and Design Markers have the largest selection of colors and types of points. At least one waterproof fine-point felt tip (like Pilot SC-UF) is a necessity. Ballpoint pens seem to be less useful because their marks are not consistent. Metallic-point pens now available (from Pilot) can

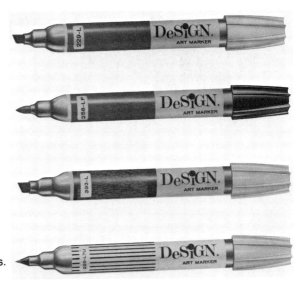

Figure 2-8
Various types of points available in fiber-tip markers.
(*Photograph courtesy Eberhard Faber*)

be useful. Leroy's Jewel-point pen can be used on plastic (acetate or mylar) surfaces. (These surfaces ruin some pen points.)

Dip pens are traditional design tools. Quills (figure 2–9), reed pens, and metal-point pens and staffs (made by Speedball, Hunt, or Gillott) give different line qualities and can be used with any kind or color of ink.

Fountain pens, which take ink up through the point and store it in the body of the pen, are easy to use and are available with many different points (figure 2–10). Osmiroid and Senator pens are available in wide ranges of nibs; these pens were traditionally able to use only water-soluble ink, but both manufacturers now make pens that can be used with permanent ink.

Figure 2-9
Speedball and Crow quill pen points and staffs.

Figure 2–10
Fountain pen with interchangeable drawing points. (*Photograph courtesy Osmiroid*)

Figure 2–11
Technical reservoir pen. (*Photograph courtesy Koh-I-Noor*)

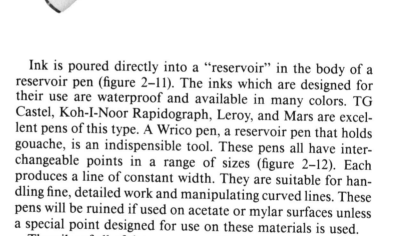

Ink is poured directly into a "reservoir" in the body of a reservoir pen (figure 2–11). The inks which are designed for their use are waterproof and available in many colors. TG Castel, Koh-I-Noor Rapidograph, Leroy, and Mars are excellent pens of this type. A Wrico pen, a reservoir pen that holds gouache, is an indispensible tool. These pens all have interchangeable points in a range of sizes (figure 2–12). Each produces a line of constant width. They are suitable for handling fine, detailed work and manipulating curved lines. These pens will be ruined if used on acetate or mylar surfaces unless a special point designed for use on these materials is used.

The nibs of all of these pens must be kept covered when not

Figure 2–12
Line-width chart of technical pen-point sizes. (*Photograph courtesy Koh-I-Noor*)

6x0	4x0	3x0	00	0	1	2	2½	3	3½	4	6	7
.13	.18	.25	.30	.35	.50	.60	.70	.80	1.00	1.20	1.40	2.00
.005 in.	.007 in.	.010 in.	.012 in.	.014 in.	.020 in.	.024 in.	.028 in.	.031 in.	.039 in.	.047 in.	.055 in.	.079 in.
.13 mm	.18 mm	.25 mm	.30 mm	.35 mm	.50 mm	.60 mm	.70 mm	.80 mm	1.00 mm	1.20 mm	1.40 mm	2.00 mm

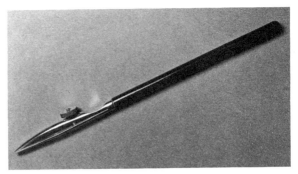

Figure 2–13
Ruling pen.

in use and must be cleaned regularly with warm water and a cleaning solution. The points are fine and become clogged very easily.

Technical pens can be stored in an improvised "humidifier" to help minimize clogging. A sponge is glued to the inside of a clean jar that will hold several pens with tip ends up. As long as the sponge is damp and the top is screwed on tightly, the pens will stay workable.

The point of a ruling pen (figure 2–13) is made of two prongs held together by a screw, which is tightened to control the thickness of line. The paint or ink is placed between the two prongs with the tip of a brush. With this indispensible tool, a designer can draw straight lines of a constant desired thickness in almost any medium. A good drawing compass (figure 2–14) with a ruling pen attachment is also necessary. Kern and Keuffel & Esser make excellent ruling pens and compasses.

Figure 2–14
Drawing compass. (*Photograph courtesy Keuffel & Esser Co.*)

Inks are available in many colors including gold and silver. As stated, restrictions exist on which inks can be used with certain pens. Acetate ink is made for use without crawling on waterproof surfaces, such as acetate and mylar. India (black waterproof) and sepia (dark brown) inks are essentials (figure 2–15). Various pen cleaners are also on the market to help dissolve waterproof inks when soap and water are not enough.

Palettes

Any glazed surface, such as a china dish, can be used as a palette. Plastic ice cube trays are excellent, but they should be white so that the color of the tray does not distort the paint color. The individual compartments of a disposable plastic palette (figure 2–16) are smaller than those of an ice cube tray, but disposable palettes are quite convenient for mixing and trying different colors. Polycon plastic paint containers (figure

Figure 2–15
Black drawing ink. (*Photograph courtesy Koh-I-Noor*)

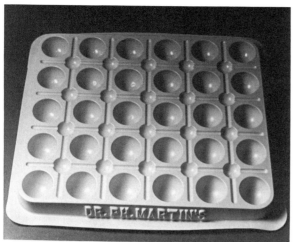

Figure 2-16
Dr. Ph. Martin's plastic palette.

Figure 2-17
Polycon plastic point saver.

2-17), which are small, individual cups with attached tops, are available in two different sizes and are perfect for mixing quantities of paint to complete an entire project. They are easy to clean because paint does not stick to the material of which they are made. Disposable individual containers are too fragile and are likely to break, even from removing and replacing the lid, before the design is completed. Plastic film containers also work well; but because they are dark, the paint color cannot be recognized except when the container is open. Pill bottles are fine also but more difficult to clean. One or two larger bowls, for mixing quantities of paint for large grounds, are also necessary.

Pencils, Sharpeners, and Erasers

Drawing pencils come in degrees of softness to hardness which are marked from 6B, which is very soft, to B, HB, F, and H to H9, which is very hard. The lead is largest in soft pencils and thinnest in hard. The leads, which are actually made largely of graphite, are available to be used in lead holders (figure 2-18). Replacing only the lead is most economical, but leads are also available encased in regular wood

Figure 2-18
Lead holder, for interchangeable leads.

pencils. Pencil extenders can be used for ease in handling small pencils. For use in mechanical pencils, 0.5 mm leads are fine enough never to need sharpening and are great for drawing layouts. Stabilio, Eagle, Eberhard Faber, Staedtler Mars, and Venus make good drawing pencils, leads, and lead holders. Working through a design, the artist can make early rough sketches with a soft lead, gradually refining using harder leads. Soft leads are used on the back of layouts for transferring the design to good paper. Additionally, leads give different types of marks. Graphite makes gray, shiny marks; a Conte or Korn litho pencil makes black, slightly greasy marks; carbon (such as Wolff's) makes matte black charcoal marks. Eagle drafting 314 pencils, Carpenter's pencils, and Koh-I-Noor soft white pencils are useful extras. Vine charcoal is used for early rough layouts.

Figure 2–19
Pointer for sharpening leads in lead holders. (*Photograph courtesy Keuffel & Esser Co.*)

It is helpful to mark different grades of lead with white tape on all sides of the pencil shaft, so that there is never a need to search through dozens of pencils for the appropriate lead.

A variety of sharpeners include a sandpaper block; a small, hand-held sharpener; and a weighted, portable pointer for mechanical pencils (figure 2–19). Emery boards and nail files can also be used. Electric sharpeners or pointers are a luxury, but without them it is amazing how much time can be spent maintaining enough sharp pencils to complete a single project. With regular wood-encased pencils, it is convenient to sharpen both ends; when one becomes dull, the other is still sharp. However, the pencil must then be marked in the middle with the lead grade.

Kneaded, gum, Pink Pearl, and ink erasers and a chamois cloth for erasing vine charcoal are necessary supplies. Staedtler Mars-Rasor (figure 2–20) looks like a mechanical pencil but holds an eraser instead of lead, and is perfect for tight, hard-to-reach spots. Also, unlike other erasers, it does not leave a shiny mark when used on a surface that is painted in gouache; and it erases on almost any surface, including photostats and film. Electric erasers have soft or hard interchangeable nibs and should be used in a gentle, rotating motion. White-out or bleed-proof white also serves as an eraser when used to cover marks. Rubber-cement thinner can be used with Q-Tips to remove grease and other tough scuff marks. Razor blades and

Figure 2–20
Staedtler Mars-Rasor, for erasing on gouache and other surfaces.

Figure 2–21
Drafting tape is specifically designed for holding paper on drawing boards. (*Photograph courtesy 3M Co.*)

Figure 2–22
Long-reach stapler allows ease in affixing designs to mount boards. (*Photograph courtesy Swingline*)

Figure 2–23
Triangle. (*Photograph courtesy Keuffel & Esser Co.*)

mat knives can be used carefully to remove heavy deposits of ink or paint. The center of a piece of bread rolled into a ball will remove smudges in an emergency.

Sheets of sandpaper from the sandpaper block are also useful to open a stubbornly closed jar. The sandpaper is wrapped around the edge of the top, rough side in, and then twisted.

Adhesives

An assortment of glues includes rubber cement and thinner in dispenser cans, Elmer's, Sobo glue, and Spray Mount. These are used as adhesives as well as for certain techniques.

Scotch transparent Magic tape and 1″ and ¼″ masking tape are basic supplies. Drafting tape is useful; it is like masking tape but tears less and, being less sticky, can be more easily removed with no damage to the paper (figure 2–21). That it is also available in white may be important for presentations. Double-coated tape can be used for display and storage of fabric swatches.

A "long-reach stapler" (figure 2–22) is necessary for stapling designs to mount boards, and a staple remover is also necessary to minimize damage to a design when a staple must be removed.

Other Essentials

Basic supplies should include a metal-edged wooden drawing board, a 24″ (or longer) steel ruler (steel is necessary for use as a cutting edge), a 9″× 12″ plastic triangle (figure 2–23), and an 18″ metal T-square with beveled edge (figure 2–24).

Good cutting tools such as a pair of sharp paper-scissors, a mat knife, and an X-Acto knife are necessary. Niji or NT Cutter multi-edge mat knives have a blade that is divided into several segments. When the first segment is dull, it can be snapped off, conveniently leaving a new, sharp blade (figure 2–25). The entire blade can be retracted into the handle when not in use.

Paint rags should always be in abundant supply. Washed cheesecloth is excellent because it is very absorbent, and a piece can be attached with a pushpin to each front corner of the drawing table so that it is always easily reached. Rolls of paper towels are also handy.

Clean water is kept in a squeeze bottle for adding to paint, as well as in a bowl or jar for dipping brushes.

Convenient color tools include a Grumbacher color wheel,

Figure 2-24
T-square. (*Photograph courtesy Keuffel & Esser Co.*)

a set of Pantone color chips, and Color-Aid paper in booklet form (figure 2–26). Paint chips from a hardware store can also be a good reference.

A small hair-dryer will save a lot of time in drying artwork but must be carefully held 12″away from the artwork surface to avoid scorching the paper or splattering the paint.

A small mirror can help to reverse or "flop" images and also show the feeling a motif will have when repeated in a textile design.

A wooden bone, available from art supply stores, can be used instead of a spoon for transferring layouts.

Some specific tools are required for stippling (also called spray effects) in painting yarn-dyed plaids. If available, an airbrush (figure 2–27) is the proper tool for best achieving this

Figure 2-25
With the Niji mat knife, when the protruding section of blade becomes dull, it can be carefully broken off, leaving a fresh, sharp section.

Figure 2-26
Color-Aid swatch book shows all shades available in Color-Aid paper and is an excellent color resource chart.

Figure 2-27
The penlike portion of an airbrush is attached by a tube to a compressor unit, through which the watercolor paint is supplied.

effect; however, natural-bristle toothbrushes (like Lactona) and a sharp paring knife can be used instead. Two brass or steel bars (12″× 2″× ¼″, from a scrap metal shop) are necessary for weighting the masked area of the design which is not to be sprayed. Frisket paper or thin acetate sprayed with Spray Mount can be used instead.

A linen tester or pick glass (figure 2–28) is a small magnifier that is used to analyze or closely inspect the surface or construction of a fabric.

Supplies are also needed for containing and transporting artwork. These should include plastic mailing tubes for rolled papers, a zippered portfolio with handles for carrying flat work, and a stiff cardboard portfolio for storage of flat work.

The Studio Setup

A textile design studio revolves around a drawing table with a surface large enough to accommodate comfortably all materials necessary for working on a large design. Materials should be to the right of the artwork if the designer is right-handed, to the left if left-handed, to avoid ever carrying a loaded brush over the artwork. Supplies may be kept on a taboret to the side of the table rather than on the work surface. Most gouache and dye work is best done on a level surface, so a tilting table is not necessary, although it may be convenient at times. Space must be allocated for flat storage of clean paper and finished designs as well as for storage of paint and small supplies. Some sort of system must be used so that all is easily located.

Good light is of paramount importance in the studio. Natural light is most pleasing but changes so dramatically that it cannot be relied upon. Likewise, customers may not view the design under natural light. A fluorescent bulb and an incandescent bulb, available combined into one lamp or as two separate lamps, should be used at the drawing table. Work should be periodically checked under natural light to be sure that it gives a good appearance under any lighting.

A light table (figure 2–29) is a very useful tool for transferring layouts, redrawing motifs, and analyzing fabric swatches. An inexpensive, portable "light table" can be obtained by attaching a piece of tracing vellum to a piece of plate glass (with smooth edges) of the same size. The edges of the glass should be thoroughly covered with strong duct or adhesive tape. One edge of the glass is placed on a table edge and the opposite side on the artist's lap with a small lamp on the floor. The "frosted" glass will thus serve as a light table.

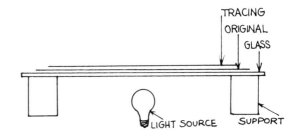

Figure 2–29
Diagram of an easily assembled light table.

Because of the expense involved, every designer will not have his own, but an opaque projector or "lucy" machine (luciograph) for reducing and enlarging images is extremely useful, as is a photocopy machine. If these are not available in the studio, the designer should make convenient and reliable arrangements for use of this equipment.

Many small tips around the studio can make work go more smoothly and easily. Bill Gray's *Complete Studio Tips* is an excellent resource for this information. Furthermore, as every designer works, he will find ways to make the situation more efficient and best suited to specific needs.

The Computer

While most original textile artwork is executed on paper, the computer has become an indispensable studio tool, and its role will surely increase. In even the smallest studio the computer has captured some design functions, and improved, more affordable features are introduced every day. Software geared to graphics use and color capabilities both on screen and as printed output allow vast new possibilities. More color combinations can be tried more quickly; repeat problems can be viewed. Nonetheless, many designers find no substitute for the variety allowed by hand-produced marks on the paper, and the "actual scale" of hand-drawn layouts. Instead, the computer helps to try more steps more quickly, increasing output (and quality) rather than replacing handwork.

3 Types of Printed Textile Designs

To appreciate the specific steps used in executing on paper the artwork called a textile design, one must be familiar with the several broad categories of design type into which trends of printed textiles will fall. It should be remembered that finished textiles are usually reproduced from drawings or paintings on paper. As types of designs are described in this chapter, observation should be made of the effects which are achieved through the use of basic textile design materials.

Variety of design may be typified by the *motifs,* or subject matter; the *style* in which the motifs are rendered; and the arrangement, or *layout,* of the motifs. These three elements, combined with the *color look* of the pattern, are the essentials that together form a textile design.

Many popular design types are derived from historical textile styles. Familiarity with the origins and history of fabric decoration not only provides understanding of the framework within which contemporary designers work but also increases access to valuable reference material. For the purposes of this discussion, however, definitions emphasize the characteristics that typify a type of design in current industrial practice rather than the historical derivation of the style.

Motifs and Styles

Florals have been the most common and best-selling printed fabrics in apparel or interior textiles for the past several hundred years. A design with flowers or other plants as motifs can be realistic or stylized. Plant drawing is difficult; therefore, many designers tend to rely on familiar, stylized floral forms. However, if used to explore, search, and render forms in a new way, an artist's drawing ability when channeled to produce unusual textile designs will be rewarded. It is important to make careful studies to see and understand how the petals grow from the stem, how leaves are attached, what components make up the center of the flower. These drawings need not result in realistic flowers completely covering a fabric, but even stylized patterns must be based on an understanding of forms in nature.

The variation of pattern that can be derived from one

flower makes it easy to understand why plant forms are such a popular design reference. The structural way that a flower grows, the complex organic shapes of which it is made, and the surprising color combinations that naturally occur keep the motifs from ever being monotonous. Equally important is the fact that most people associate no negative connotations with flowers as they might with some sort of animal, for example. Whether or not a particular design style becomes unpopular, some interpretation of plant forms, whether abstract, stylized, or realistic, will always be prevalent.

The existence of *chintz*, from the Hindu word *chint,* meaning colored or variegated, was recorded as early as 400 B.C. Through centuries of dyed and printed fabric development in India, the term was used to describe many types of pattern. The floral motifs, in various arrangements, were rendered in a particular style popular in Europe, especially France and England, during specific historical periods. Today, a chintz is usually thought of as a home furnishing–scale floral pattern; a typical example is shown in figure 3–1. The colors of the motifs are usually strong and vibrant, often in striking contrast to a very light, very dark, or very rich blotch color. Ivory,

Figure 3–1
Kabuki, all-overfloral on dark ground, print on cotton.
(© *P. Kaufmann, Inc.*)

navy, black, burgundy, and lacquer red are popular blotch colors in chintzes. The glazed or polished finish that is usually applied to these cotton fabrics after they are printed may also be applied to fabrics that are dyed a solid color. Such a fabric, although not a printed design at all, is often referred to as a chintz.

Winding, unending bouquets profusely covering the design surface, sometimes utilizing symmetrical motifs, typify florals done by the master craftsman William Morris in the late 1800s. Patterns that resemble Morris' and his pupils' designs remain a style in their own right; many William Morris designs are reproduced and sold today exactly as they were during his lifetime.

Morris was a prolific designer, craftsman, poet, and social reformer, and his work spanned several decades. His designs for fabrics varied in style, certainly, as his career progressed. The example shown in figure 3–2, however, shows the carefully drawn floral forms richly embellishing the textile surface,

Figure 3–2
Honeysuckle pattern by William Morris, printed cotton, English, 19th century. (*The Metropolitan Museum of Art, The Theodore M. Davis Collection, Bequest of Theodore M. Davis, 1915. 30.95.45*)

Figure 3–3
Howqua's Garden, botanical print on cotton. (© *Brunschwig & Fils, Inc.*)

characteristics found in most of Morris's work. His textiles feature subtle, grayed colors. The penlike lines providing an etched quality are also typical.

In a *botanical,* entire plant forms are realistically rendered as if the viewer were seeing each part of the form at eye level, as in a botanical illustration. These motifs may be repeated in the pattern as completely separate elements, and even boxed off from one another. The plant species may even be labeled as a part of the design. Figure 3–3 shows a traditional botanical, while figure 3–4 illustrates more stylized motifs worked in a botanical layout.

The deeply colored florals on light grounds shown in figures 3–5 and 3–6 are printed *Jacobean* designs, derived from popular embroidered furnishing fabrics of the late Elizabethan and Jacobean eras. Characterized by heavy ornament of German and Flemish origin, these patterns are usually made up of branches and other arborescent forms accented by floral motifs.

The small-scale floral patterns in figures 3–7, 3–8, and 3–9 are *Provençal,* or country-French, designs which originated during the eighteenth century in the district of southern France called Provence and today are popular in both apparel and home furnishings. Originally wood block patterns, the slightly off-register color placement in these designs is part of their charm. Rich colors such as Wedgwood blue, yellow ochre, and poppy red are used together in vibrating combinations. The

41

Figure 3–4 (left)
Korin, stylized botanical print on cotton. (© Jay Yang Designs Ltd.)

Figure 3–5 (below left)
Jacobean Tree, print on cotton. (© Lee Jofa, photograph courtesy Lee Jofa)

Figure 3–6 (below right)
Le Forêt Imaginaire, Jacobean print on cotton. (© Brunschwig & Fils, Inc.)

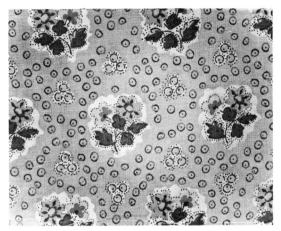

Figure 3-7 *(above left)*
Provençal design, print on cotton. (© *Pierre Deux*)

Figure 3-8 *(above right)*
Provençal design, print on cotton. (© *Pierre Deux*)

Figure 3-9 *(right)*
Provençal design, print on cotton. (© *Pierre Deux*)

small floral motifs typifying these designs are very regularly spaced and may be designed as borders and stripes which coordinate.

In addition to flowers, other natural forms such as animals, shells, stones, waves, and landscapes are traditionally popular motifs in textiles (figures 3–10, 3–11). Historical landscape or scenic patterns include *chinoiserie* designs from the mid-1700s, many of which were printed at the famous print works at Jouy, France, and are therefore called *toile de Jouy* (which means cloth from Jouy). These designs, such as in figure 3–12, were usually printed in one color on a natural ground, and used complete pastoral or figurative "pictures" as motifs in simple repeats (figure 3–13). Toiles also encompass one-color florals, which feature vine-traversed layouts with large exposed areas of the natural ground cloth.

Chinoiserie is used today to refer to any Western interpre-

43

Figure 3–10
Seashells, metallic gold pigment on tracing paper. (© *1983 Almuth Palin-kas photograph courtesy of the artist*)

Figure 3–11
Butti and *Butti Stripe,* Jacquard woven toile design. (© *Pollack & Associates, photograph Maryanne Solensky*)

Figure 3–13
Pastorale design, print on cotton/viscose. (© *Cantoni Satilai, Spa.*)

Figure 3–12
Copperplate print on cotton, *toile,* English, circa 1780. *(The Metropolitan Museum of Art, Rogers Fund, 1923. 23.2.6)*

Figure 3-14
Kang Hsi, Chinoiserie design, print on cotton. (© *Jay Yang Designs Ltd.*)

tation of oriental design. This influence may be shown in the style of floral rendering, but more often a chinoiserie contains figurative clues. Chinese architectural elements (such as a pagoda), the Chinese vases and ornament shown in the textile in figure 3–14, or stereotypical Chinese plant forms such as the bamboo used in the design in figure 3–15 accent floral or figurative motifs in these designs.

Designs that use pictures of recognizable objects making up the pattern are called *conversationals* or, in Europe,

Figure 3-15
China Grove, chinoiserie design, print on cotton. (© *P. Kaufmann, Inc.*)

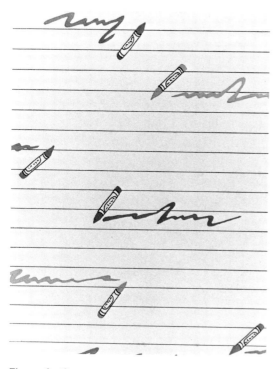

Figure 3–16
Conversational design, gouache on paper. (© *N.J. Cohen*)

Figure 3–17
Bo Boo, juvenile design, print on cotton. (© *Marimekko 1975*)

figuratives. Motifs used in conversationals range from the crayons in figure 3–16 to seashells and even to people. They may be oriented toward any segment of the market; *juvenile* patterns, designed to be used for children's products, are often conversationals. *Juveniles,* whether featuring the cars shown in figure 3–17, animals, balloons, clowns or other popular motifs, are usually boldly drawn and brightly colored.

Geometrics, derived from any geometric shape, are the most prevalent type of design other than florals. As figure 3–18 illustrates, a geometric may simply feature lines arranged on a single ground color. Or, ranging to much more elaborate designs, paisleys, though originally derived from curved leaf forms, are often stylized and isolated to yield the effect of a geometric pattern, as illustrated in figures 3–19 and 3–20.

Contemporary is a term used in the interior textile area to classify simple geometrics or designs with simple, extremely stylized motifs. Calligraphic brushstrokes, as shown in figure 3–21, are typical contemporary motifs.

Transitional designs are almost contemporary, but the styl-

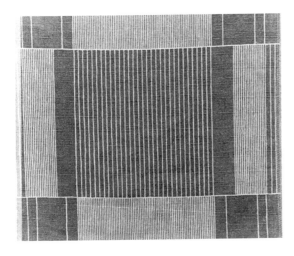

Figure 3–18
Greece, geometric design, monotone print on flame retardant polyester. (© *Charles Samelson, Inc., American licensee for Pausa*)

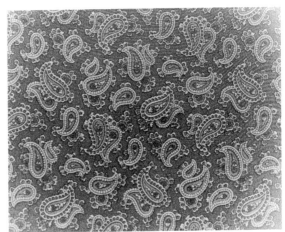

Figure 3–19
Paisley design, tossed layout, print on silk. (© *Ratti*)

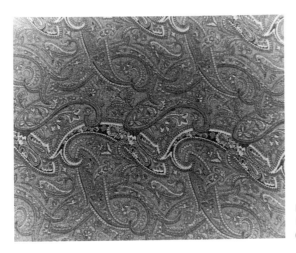

Figure 3–20
Paisley design, set layout, print on cotton/viscose. (© *Cantoni Satilai*)

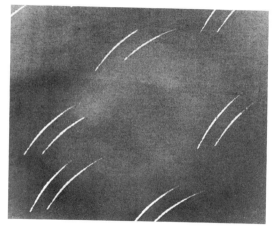

Figure 3–21
Shadow, contemporary design, print on cotton. (© *Knoll International, Adrian Parry Collection*)

Figure 3–22
Transitional design, rayon/cotton Jacquard fabric. (© *Craftex Mills of Pa.*)

ized motifs are not as starkly simple and may have recognizable naturalistic motifs. Where a contemporary pattern would be suitable only on very simple furniture, a transitional upholstery pattern could be used to update a more traditional piece. Figures 3–22 and 3–23 show floral and leaf forms rendered as brushstroke-like marks to yield this bridge between realistic and completely non-figurative designs. *Transitional* is also

Figure 3–23
Transitional design, rayon/cotton Jacquard fabric. (© *Craftex Mills of Pa.*)

used as a catch-all term for interior textile floral patterns that do not represent any particular historical style, and can, in theory, be used in any setting or on any style of furniture.

Trompe l'oeil (pronounced trōⁿp-lœi) in French literally means "to fool the eye," and patterns so designated create such an effect. By carefully rendering objects in extremely fine detail and emphasizing the illusion of tactile and spacial qualities, *trompe l'oeil* designs, as shown in figures 3–24 and 3–25, are most often used in interiors to simulate marble surfaces or to depict absent architectural features, such as columns or arches.

Throughout the history of printed textiles, patterns were developed to emulate more expensive woven techniques. In addition to simple stripes, plaids, twills, and herringbones, more complex fabric structures such as tapestry, brocade, damask, and even Persian rugs continue to influence printed pattern.

Likewise, special dying methods are simulated in printed

Figure 3–25
Canna, detail (© *Mira-X*)

Figure 3–24
Mira-Marmoreus, design *Canna*, *trompe l'oeil* design, print on cotton. (H Design, Robert & Trix Haussmann, Alfred Habluetzel for Mira-X International Furnishings, Inc.)

Figure 3-26
Lyon chiné à la brance, French, 18th century. (*The Metropolitan Museum of Art, Rogers Fund, 1935. 35.98.4a*)

Figure 3-27
Vezalay, simulated ikat/*chiné* effect, print on cotton. (© *Jay Yang Designs Ltd.*)

patterns. Figure 3–26 shows an actual warp-printed *chiné* fabric; figure 3–27 is a printed-fabric version of this technique. Hand-painted effects, fabrics with resist-dyed warps (such as Japanese *kasuri* and Indonesian *ikat*), Japanese *shibori* (tie dye) techniques, and the Indonesian wax-resist dyed batik designs shown in 3–28 and 3–29 are all techniques simulated through printing. (The warp-printing techniques mentioned here are further discussed on page 103.)

Textiles from different cultures influence ethnic designs. African inspiration, as shown in the geometrics in 3–30 and 3–31; Early American influence; the Chinese and Japanese influences previously discussed; and any other culture may contribute motifs, patterns, and techniques popular in various styles of design. Likewise, patterns from art or architectural movements, such as art deco, art nouveau, op, and postmodern, work their way into textiles.

A *documentary* is a design derived from a specific style or even a certain fabric. A designer may take a group of fabrics

Figure 3–28
Leaves of Grass, batik on cotton velvet. (© *Jack Lenor Larsen, Inc., photograph courtesy Jack Lenor Larsen, Inc.*)

Figure 3–29
Leaves, border design, watercolor on paper simulating batik effect. (© *1980 Almuth Palinkas, photograph courtesy of the artist*)

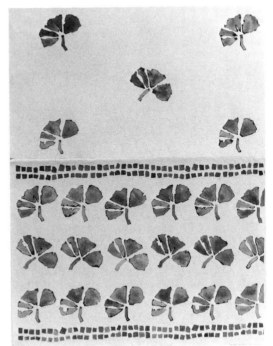

Figure 3–30
Caravan, African-inspired design by Anita Askild & Larsen Design, print on cotton velvet. (© *1962 Jack Lenor Larsen, Inc.*)

from a museum and develop up-to-date patterns from the historic textiles. The new pattern may be a loose interpretation of the document; however, if the new design is very close to the original, the original is given credit. Often a museum licenses the right to reproduce textiles from its collection as well as the museum's name. The museum then oversees the development of such designs for commercial uses. Figure 3–32 shows a handpainted silk panel from the eighteenth century that was developed into the twentieth-century repeat pattern shown in figure 3–33.

Coordinates are designs developed to be used together. A geometric may be a coordinate to a floral, as illustrated in 3–34 and 3–35, or some of the motifs in a floral may be put into a different scale or layout to make a coordinate. A stripe may go with a plaid or check, or one pattern may be rendered in two techniques to give a slightly different look. A group of coordinates developed and presented as a "story" will sell more easily than a sole pattern, although good coordinate patterns will stand on their own as individually successful designs.

Figure 3–31
Akwete, Kumasi, Igarra, African-inspired designs, prints on cotton. (© *Lee Jofa, photograph courtesy Lee Jofa*)

Figure 3–32
Samarkand, print on cotton. (© *P. Kaufmann, Inc., photograph Mikio Sekita*)

Figure 3–33
(Left) *Le Route du Mandarin,* print on cotton, design developed from original
document, 18th-century handpainted silk panel (right). *(Photographs courtesy
Clarence House Fabrics Ltd.)*

Figure 3–34
Floral design in tossed layout, gouache on paper. (© *1980
Marypaul Yates*)

Figure 3–35
Geometric design in stripe layout, gouache on
paper, developed as a coordinate pattern to Fig.
3–34. (© *1980 Marypaul Yates*)

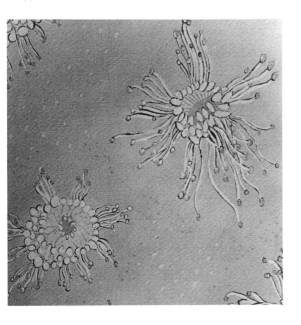 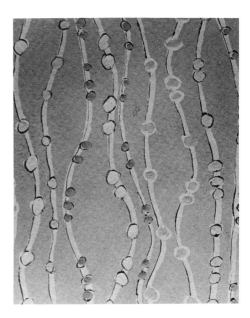

Layouts

Textile design types may be categorized by layout as well as by motif or style of pattern. The term *layout* refers to the arrangement of motifs in the framework of the design plane. Unlike a painting or drawing, which is designed in relation to its boundaries or edges, the elements in a textile design are designed in relation only to each other. There are no boundaries; when the pattern is printed, it will continue over yards and yards of cloth.

For a textile design to be reproduced on fabric, it must eventually be developed into one standard unit containing a specific arrangement of the desired motifs. This one unit, called a repeat, will be repeated across the width and length of the fabric in a continuous manner.

Designs are sometimes done in repeat from the start but are often designed in balance and put in repeat later. A balanced design, called a *croquis* (the French word, pronounced krō-′kē, means sketch), must give the feeling that would be evoked if a frame were placed at random over any one section of the finished length of cloth. The same feeling should be evoked if the frame were placed on any section even though the sections were not identical. Although not in repeat, a croquis will have the feeling of being in repeat; the motifs and colors are arranged with no "line-ups" (unintentional lines formed with motifs, as shown in figure 3–36), "alleyways" (unintentional lines formed by negative spaces, as shown in figure 3–37), or "holes" (uneven gaps between motifs, as shown in figure 3–38).

Any specific motif will recur on the fabric at measured

Figure 3–36 *(below left)*
The dashed lines in the drawing show unintentional lines formed by the edges of certain motifs within a croquis.

Figure 3–37 *(below center)*
The dashed lines in the drawing show unintentional lines formed by the negative spaces within a croquis.

Figure 3–38 *(below right)*
If a design featuring motifs positioned as shown in this drawing were repeated on fabric, the irregular space with no motif would seem to be a flaw in the fabric.

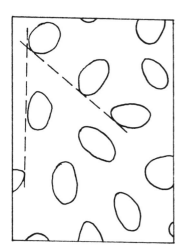

intervals because each motif holds a specific location within the repeat unit, and the entire unit is printed over and over again above itself, below itself, and beside itself, thus covering the fabric. Within the repeat unit itself, however, the motifs may be of any density; and a variety of density is both more natural and more dynamic. Within the repeat unit, motifs do not need to be evenly spaced. Whether close together or far apart, they must have a consistent relationship to each other. When the design unit is continued over the fabric, one motif or space viewed as distinct from all the others will look like a mistake. It is the subtle differences in motifs and spacing that will make a design interesting.

A pattern composed of motifs that do not recur at regular, measured intervals within one repeat unit of the design is referred to as a *tossed* pattern. These elements may be spaced (with ground area between motifs, as in figure 3–39) or packed (so that motifs touch, as in figure 3–40) but are separated by ground area. Similarly, an *all-over* layout has balanced motifs that recur irregularly within the repeat unit; the difference is

Figure 3–39
Conversational design in tossed layout, one-color print on cotton.
(© *Cantoni Satilai*)

Figure 3–40
Floral design in packed layout, print on cotton/viscose.
(© *Cantoni Satilai*)

Figure 3–41
Mitsuko, floral design in all-over layout, print on cotton. (© *Jay Yang Designs Ltd.*)

that the motifs are connected in some way, forming a network that covers the entire design plane, as shown in figures 3–41 and 3–42. Typical of the William Morris and Jacobean periods, a Tree of Life, shown in figure 3–43, is a type of all-over layout (also called a *meander*). These designs feature elaborate, embellished floral-like motifs that seem to grow and wander across the design plane.

A pattern in which all motifs repeat directly under and directly across from one another at measured intervals is called a *set* or *tailored* pattern. Small patterns of this type are

Figure 3–42
Organic shapes in all-over layout, gouache on paper.

Figure 3–43
L'Arbre Exotique, tree of life design (meander), all-over layout, print on cotton. (© *Brunschwig & Fils, Inc.*)

also called *foulards,* which is the French word for the silk or rayon fabrics for neckties and scarves often printed with these patterns, as shown in figures 3–44 and 3–45. Polka dots, for example, are a set pattern.

Flowers or plants can be arranged in what is called a *bouquet* layout, with identical or varying bouquets usually repeating at regular intervals, as in figure 3–46. A five-point bouquet is a layout arranged so that, when the fabric is cut to

Figure 3–44
Foulard design (set layout), print on cotton/viscose. (© *Cantoni Satilai*)

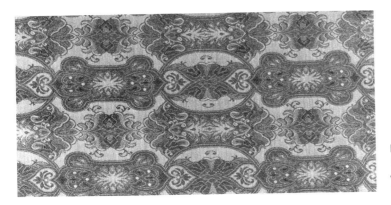

Figure 3–45
Colonade, foulard design (set layout), Jacquard woven. (© *Arc-Com Fabrics, photograph courtesy Arc-Com*)

Figure 3–46
Floral in bouquet layout, monotone print on cotton. (© *Cantoni Satilai*)

cover a sofa cushion, one bouquet is in the center and a quarter of a bouquet shows at each corner of the cushion.

A once popular format rarely used today except in wallpaper and traditional damask patterns (although it was used often in William Morris' designs), is the *ogee* layout, which utilizes onion-shaped motifs. The textile illustrated in 3–47 shows how the "points" of the onions fit together to form the structure of the design. This type of pattern almost always

Figure 3–47
Mariguan Damask, design in ogee layout, rayon/cotton Jacquard fabric. (© *Brunschwig & Fils, Inc.*)

features floral forms in urns or vases as well as birds as motifs; the damask and wallpaper designs in this layout are almost always of a single color on a contrasting ground.

A horizontal stripe layout is called a *bayadere* (pronounced bī-ə-di[ə]r). As the design in figure 3–48 shows, this need not be simply a geometric stripe composed of straight lines, but may feature any type of motif arranged in a horizontal format. While a bayadere is possible with any type of printing, vertical stripe layouts are not possible in flat-bed screen printing (further discussed on page 98) due to the difficulty of matching up the stripes from one screen to another during printing.

Diagonal stripes, common in home furnishings, are almost always at a 45° angle, not only for ease in matching the design at the seams, but also for use either horizontally or vertically. The diagonal usually runs from lower left to upper right.

A *border* pattern, as in figure 3–49, is focused along one selvedge with a ground extending to the other selvedge. A border fabric is used for garments (or draperies) with a border

Figure 3–48
Clearwater, bayadere layout, print on cotton velvet. (© *Jack Lenor Larsen, Inc.*)

Figure 3–49
Geometric design in border layout, *tjanting* and watercolor on *masa* paper. (© *N.J. Cohen*)

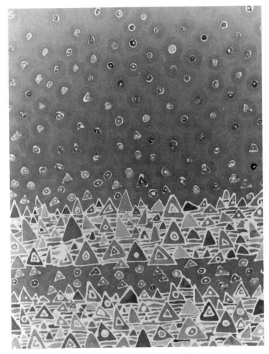

around the hem; therefore, enough space must be allowed in the design for the hem of the skirt or dress to be turned under without distorting the design.

Some home furnishings fabrics are designed so that there is a border along each selvedge with the ground in between, forming in essence a double border. When one screen makes the entire, completely self-contained pattern, it is referred to as an *engineered pattern.* Designed almost like a drawing or painting, engineered patterns are striking in pillow cases, towels, area rugs, and scarves (as shown in figure 3–51).

In any type of layout, whether it is engineered, ogee, bouquet, etc., the direction of the motifs must be considered. In a one-way pattern (figure 3–52) all the motifs face upright in the same direction. In a two-way pattern (figure 3–53) half the motifs face upright and half are upside down so that the pattern gives the same feeling in either vertical direction. Fabrics printed with one-way or two-way patterns, however, must always be utilized in a consistent direction. That is, fabrics so printed must always be cut with respect to the "top" and "bottom" of the pattern so that a piece of fabric showing upside-down motifs is not placed next to a piece showing rightside-up motifs. Because direction of motifs is a consideration in the utilization of these patterns, they are referred to as *directional.*

By contrast, in a multidirectional pattern (3–54), where motifs face all directions, the pattern looks correct from any angle, pieces of fabric can be used together in any way, and therefore the pattern is essentially *non-directional.*

One-way patterns (either vertical or horizontal) are easily utilized for upholstery fabric and are therefore common in designs for this area. Horizontal patterns, when used for upholstery fabric, are usually "railroaded"; that is, the fabric is turned sideways so that the direction of the pattern runs vertically on the furniture. Vertical one-way or two-way patterns are likewise convenient formats for drapery fabrics, but most American drapery manufacturers are unwilling to spend

Figure 3–52
Design in one-way layout, marker on *masa* paper. (© *1982 Marypaul Yates*)

Figure 3–53
Design in two-way layout, marker on *masa* paper. (© *1982 Marypaul Yates*)

Figure 3–54
Design in multidirectional (non-directional) layout, marker on *masa* paper. (© *1982 Marypaul Yates*)

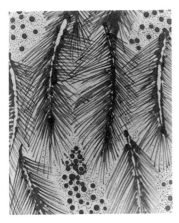

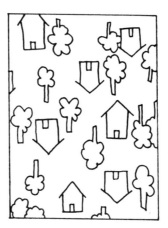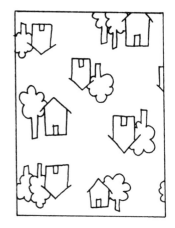

Figure 3–55
Although the spacing of motifs in the layout on the left seems reasonable, the design is confusing because houses are next to upside-down trees. The arrangement on the right solves this layout problem.

the extra time and care required to line up horizontally positioned patterns at the seams (called "side matching" the pattern). Therefore, horizontal drapery patterns are uncommon in this country unless the shapes are unspecific enough that precise side matching is not required. European drapery manufacturers are more willing to handle this extra labor, and horizontal stripes are more common.

For clothing, however, because the shapes and sizes of pieces of fabric making up a garment vary more than the standard rectangles making up furniture and windows, more fabric and more careful planning are needed in order to use a directional pattern wisely. Apparel customers may therefore shy away from patterns that look correct from only one direction.

In a figurative two-way or multidirectional pattern for any end use, the images must be logical. For example, if there are houses next to trees, the trees and the house are flipped together, not just the trees or just the houses (figure 3–55).

The Process of Designing Printed Fabric

4

This chapter is devoted to introducing a basic guideline for developing and refining an idea into a complete textile pattern, as in figure 4–1.

Simple formats that show the design at each stage are convenient for the student of textile design as well as professional members of the industry. Delineation at each stage of the design process allows a designer to keep accurate records, which can be shown to customers or other personnel involved in the project.

In this chapter, concentration is placed on designing in croquis form; patterns in repeat will be discussed later.

Figure 4–1
Carmella, floral design, bouquet layout, print on cotton. (© *Cyrus Clark, photograph Mikio Sekita*)

The Rough Layout

In pencil, on large pieces of tracing paper (approximately 3′ × 3′), a right angle is squared off in the upper left corner, leaving ample room outside the angle as a margin. Because the paper is translucent and is constantly turned around and over during work, it is easy to lose orientation; therefore, "Top Front" is always marked above the right angle to keep a point of reference. The motifs may be drawn on these sheets of paper to show different ideas, arrangements, interpretations, sizes, and types of layouts (figure 4–2).

Vine charcoal is an excellent medium in which to work because it can be easily erased with a chamois cloth, allowing the artist to change and develop drawings. A soft lead pencil is also good. Some designers begin these rough drawings on bond paper before working on tracing paper, which being inexpensive allows a lot of change without concern for cost of materials.

Although it is a good idea to make some small sketches of ideas, it is extremely important to start drawings on a large

Figure 4–2
A rough layout shows approximate position and direction of motifs.

scale and refine down if necessary. The freshness and loose-
ness of a large drawing can be maintained as the size is
diminished, but the enlargement of a small drawing usually
looks fussy. A comfortably large drawing has an additional
importance in home furnishings, where final designs are often
27″× 27″ or even larger.

Through these rough layout sketches, one version of the
idea that seems to work best will be chosen and then refined
to a polished form. The "polished layout" is a perfect drawing.
When rendered and painted, it will be the final artwork. The
rough layouts are in a size that is comfortable for loose, quick
sketches, but the polished drawing should be the exact size of
the final presentation.

The Arrangement of Motifs

The arrangement of motifs as established in the rough
layout cannot be regarded casually. Dynamic composition
within a pattern can be achieved with distinction between
design elements and recurrence of motifs just as it can be
achieved through color and painting technique. Designing
motifs in relation to one another rather than in relation to
boundaries is a compositional problem peculiar to textile
design; it is, in fact, the essence of flat pattern design. Consummate skill in layout is probably the distinguishing characteristic of master textile surface designers. Important layout
differences that may not be noticeable at first glance may be
the precise elements providing the verve in a particular pattern. Such layouts are better appreciated on interior textiles
than on apparel textiles; their distinctive qualities are more
obvious when placed on simple and stationary pieces of furniture as opposed to the small shapes that make up clothing.
Layouts for interior textiles are, therefore regarded more carefully, but, needless to say, layouts for apparel fabrics must also
be thoughtfully designed.

Establishing Design Size

Design size is determined by three factors: the size of the
motifs and space, the desired end use of the fabric, and the
equipment that the particular company uses.

To give the overall feeling of clothing on a person, apparel
croquis are developed in a vertical format. (The exception is
a bayadere; because it is on a horizontal axis, the design may
need to have a more horizontal format to show the entire
pattern.) In apparel, the motifs are usually relatively small,

65

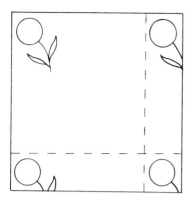

Figure 4–3

Decorative designs are rendered so that one entire repeat unit, and a portion of the adjacent units on the right and bottom, will be shown in the final design.

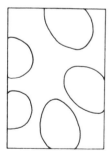

Figure 4–4

A croquis should show each different motif at least once in the drawing, although some motifs will run off the edges. Layouts such as the one shown here are a problem because no motif is shown in its entirety. A customer cannot properly judge the design, the type of spacing, or the motifs.

since a large pattern will often look choppy when the fabric is made into clothing, unless careful planning is used to engineer the fabric pattern to the garment. Apparel fabrics are designed in croquis form so that many ideas can be developed quickly, and those that are chosen to be printed are put into repeat. Repeat sizes vary, and particular companies use different types of printing equipment.

Because upholstery, drapery, and wall covering have standard repeat sizes, these fabrics are usually designed in repeat. The repeat sizes for these uses are larger than those in apparel, and the motifs also are commonly larger since the fabric is used in large amounts and as simple shapes in the finished product. When these designs are developed in repeat, the entire repeat plus the beginning of the new repeat on the right side and bottom are usually shown, as illustrated in figure 4–3.

Fabrics for other specific uses will have specific repeat sizes, such as those for towels, pillow cases, and sheets. Specific dimensions are covered in the chapter on repeats; at this point the scale of the motifs as it relates to the desired end product should be the main consideration.

It is important to remember that *all* the information about the design must be shown clearly and consistently in a croquis. The drawing must be large enough to show how the design elements recur in relation to one another. For clarity, each different motif must be shown in its entirety at least once in the croquis, although there will be motifs running off the edges of the croquis. A croquis that has *all* the motifs running off the edge is sometimes called "French" (figure 4–4). This should be avoided; if a customer (the fabric manufacturer) cannot get an accurate feel for the images, layout, technique, and color, he will reject the design.

A designer in a particular area normally works in one of a few standard sizes of design formats. Rather than measuring off the design size each time, it is, therefore, convenient to keep pieces of tracing paper marked with these standard rectangles to be easily traced or transferred. If the artist is designing in repeat rather than croquis form, the rectangle of the required repeat size is completely drawn in the beginning. The rough layout is refined as much as possible, generously showing adjacent repeats so that recurrence of motifs in the surrounding units may be borne in mind. To anticipate problem areas, it may also be useful to draw small sketches indicating placement of motifs. Later, when the polished layout is completed, one repeat unit, with the beginning of the next repeat on the right side and bottom, will be transferred to the good paper.

Drawing the Motifs

Once design size is established, the motifs should be drawn in pencil on a new piece of tracing paper exactly as they will be used. These motifs do not necessarily need to be drawn in the format of a layout; in fact, it may be useful to cut each motif apart from the rest so that they can be rearranged slightly as the process continues. Photocopies of individual motifs may aid in placement of identical elements within the final layout.

It should be remembered that motifs that are intended to be identical must be exactly that; slight differences will be viewed as errors. This does not mean, however, that all the flowers must be rendered identically or that all the leaves must look exactly alike. A flower may be viewed from different angles, showing different characteristics each time. Leaves may bend and curve differently. Again, subtlety adds realism and interest to the pattern. Nevertheless, differences must be intentional and not merely the result of poor draftsmanship or sloppy execution of technique and painting.

Refining the Layout

To begin the polished layout, the top left reference angle is again squared off on a new piece of tracing paper, which is marked "Top Front." The lines from the right angle are continued to mark the exact size and shape of the layout (a 10″× 12″ rectangle, for example), again leaving a large margin around the format. The rough layout, which has been refined as much as possible, is placed under this new piece of tracing paper; the top left right angles are aligned, and both pieces of paper are anchored to the work surface with masking or drafting tape.

Next, the drawn individual motifs are placed between the rough layout and the new piece of paper (see figure 4–5). With the rough layout as a guide for positioning the motifs, a final check should be made. The arrangement of the motifs must be balanced; there should be no alleyways, line ups, or holes. Slight readjustments may be necessary, especially in scaling the rough layout to the proportions of the final design size.

Once the arrangement is correct, the small, loose pieces of paper are attached with transparent tape to the rough layout, or to the back of the new piece of paper (see figure 4–5). The motifs are drawn and traced onto the new paper. Even if it crosses the outside edge of the design, the entire motif should be drawn.

67

Figure 4-5
Loose motifs are positioned, using the rough layout as a guide, and then traced onto a clean piece of tracing paper.

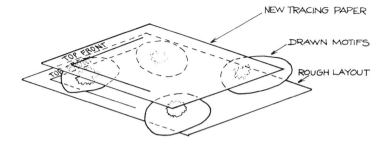

NEW TRACING PAPER

DRAWN MOTIFS

ROUGH LAYOUT

TOP FRONT

TOP

Figure 4-6 *(below left)*
The polished layout developed from the rough layout in fig. 4-2 shows a precise line drawing of the pattern being designed.

Figure 4-7 *(below right)*
The complete croquis, developed from the polished layout in fig. 4-6, was in this case painted in gouache on cold pressed watercolor paper. (© *1981 Marypaul Yates*)

Because the rough edges of the art papers and the tapes may be distracting in finalizing the placement of motifs, it is a good idea to make a quick tracing outlining the motifs to be viewed separately. More adjustments may be necessary before completing the polished layout.

Once this working drawing is perfected, it will be transferred to "good" paper—the ground paper on which the final design will be rendered. This polished layout is a finished line drawing of the fabric being designed; it should be a clear image of how the actual fabric will look (figures 4-6, 4-7, 4-8, and 4-9).

Layouts should be saved for reference. A similar layout may be used with different motifs, or the same motifs may be used in a different arrangement. The polished layout, painted swatches of the colors actually used, and a snapshot of the finished design provide an excellent record of the design for records or for a possible emergency, for instance, loss of the design by the customer.

Technique and Color

It is possible to complete the polished layout drawing without giving any thought to the color of the design. More often than not, however, from the beginning a designer has some idea how the final artwork will look with regard to colors. Once the polished layout is complete, experimentation with various media and techniques will begin, resulting in a specific plan for the final artwork.

Approaches to this problem are covered thoroughly in the chapters on Techniques and Color Combination. In this chapter, concentration is placed on the formats in which ideas and work are developed and presented. Certain basics, however,

Figure 4–8
Wildwood, scenic, designed by Wendy Klein, one-way pattern, ink on paper. (© *Jack Lenor Larsen, Inc., photograph courtesy of the artist*)

Figure 4–9
Elements Collection, stripe, meander floral, and abstract texture, prints on Trevira polyester. (© *Arc-Com Fabrics, photograph courtesy Arc-Com)*)

must be kept in mind. For one, there is always a maximum number of colors allowable per design—usually six for apparel and eight to twelve for decorative. Because each color is printed with an individual screen, each color increases the cost of production. Wherever one color appears in the design, it must be consistently the same color. In the actual fabric, each individual color is produced by one dye paste, which colors every area on the fabric that is intended to be that color. There will be no variation in this color, wherever it appears on the cloth. In the painted design, therefore, it is equally important that each color have no variation. Another critical factor is color efficiency. Two colors that are so close in hue that the difference is not noticeable from a distance will not justify the cost of two screens. Furthermore, color choices should be appropriate for the market; that is, colors must be suitable for the season and the end use. Color sells the fabric; there is always a customer for a great color look. Nevertheless, the tastes and requirements of the market for which the design is intended must be kept in mind.

Color Roughs

After one of the color and technique looks is chosen from this experimentation, the layout of the color must be established in the design. On a new piece of tracing paper over the polished layout, color is "spotted in," using any convenient medium. Just as the rough layout was used to develop balance of motifs and space, this tracing paper showing potential color placement is called a "color rough" and will show color balance (figure 4–10). For example, all blue flowers should not be placed in one area of the design but evenly distributed in the croquis.

The Color and Technique Plan

Using this color rough and the ideas from the color and technique experimentation, the designer produces an exact

Figure 4-10
A color rough is developed by placing a clean sheet of tracing paper over the polished layout and sketching in spots of color to assure that the design will have proper color distribution.

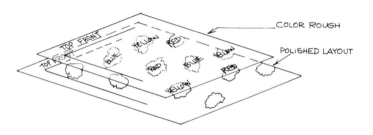

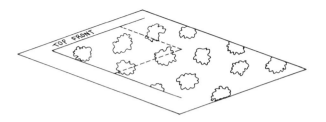

Figure 4-11
A section of the layout (perhaps the upper left corner) is transferred to the design paper and rendered in the intended colors and technique of the final design.

painted rendering of the planned design in technique and color. For this plan, a section is chosen from the upper left-hand corner of the polished layout or from an area that encompasses the full range of color and technique within the design, always keeping the image square with the layout (figure 4–11). This *color and technique plan*, made on the same kind of paper that will be used for the final artwork, later becomes the *color plate*, that is, the format for further colorways. This original plan is often referred to as the "*document colorway*," particularly if the design was adapted from an actual historical document.

This step allows the artist to work out any technical difficulties that may arise. When this exact color and technique plan is complete, he should be comfortable with all the materials necessary to execute the final artwork (see figures 4–12, 4–13, and 4–14).

Transferring the Layout

Once all plans are made and the designer is sure of the color and techniques that will be used, the finished layout must be taken from the tracing paper and drawn on the ground paper chosen for the final artwork.

Figure 4-12
Floral design, packed layout, gouache on paper. (© 1982 Almuth Palinkas, photograph courtesy of the artist)

Figure 4-13
Polished layout for Floral border, border layout, ink and pencil on tracing paper. (© 1983 Almuth Palinkas, photograph courtesy of the artist)

Figure 4-14
Floral border, border layout, gouache on paper. (© 1983 Almuth Palinkas, photograph courtesy of the artist)

There are several methods of transferring the polished layout to the design paper. The most common is the rub-down method. First, the design is *backed* (figure 4-15). The polished layout is turned face down, covered with a new piece of tracing paper; both are taped together to the work surface. Then, with a soft lead pencil, the back of the polished layout is exactly traced. The outside boundaries of the design must be traced as well. After the entire design is traced, one corner of the "backing" should be lifted to check that no motifs were omitted before the papers are untaped.

Next, the design is burnished, or rubbed down (figure 4-16). The good paper should be taped to the work surface, the new reverse layout placed mark side down over the good paper, and then the layout taped to the work surface. A spoon is used to rub across the layout, transferring the marks on the back of the tracing paper to the good paper. (A wooden bone from an art supply store can be used instead of a spoon. It is comfortable to hold and does not make the irritating sound that a spoon makes.) The spoon must always be moved in the same direction, using short strokes to avoid tearing the tracing paper. Again, one corner of the tracing paper should be lifted first to check to see that no motifs were omitted.

Figure 4-15 (below left)
The polished layout is "backed" by being placed face-down and every line traced through the paper onto the back of the layout (or onto a clean sheet of paper that is placed over the face-down layout).

Figure 4-16 (below right)
The backed layout is placed on the design paper, and the drawing transferred by rubbing the face of the layout with a spoon or wooden bone.

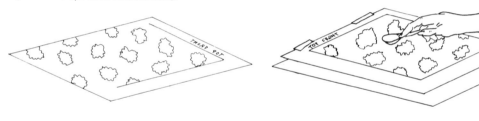

The rub-down method is the most popular transfer method because the marks on the good paper are completely erasable; and since the good paper is not marked directly, there are no indentations from the drawn lines, which sometimes show through paint. If the paint is translucent, as in watercolor dyes, this is a special consideration.

When transferring a layout to a dark or colored piece of paper, using a sharp white pencil to back the design is convenient. Burnishing might damage the colored paper. If a test determines that the paper will be damaged, the backed layout should be placed right side up over the colored paper and each motif retraced so that the white line on the back is transferred to the colored paper. This technique may also be used to transfer a design to a ground painted in gouache, which, except for a light to medium shade, may also be damaged by burnishing.

In some cases it is not necessary to back the design or use any transfer paper when transferring to a painted or colored ground that is soft enough to show clear indentation lines from pencil marks. The designer simply tapes the polished layout over the ground paper and retraces each motif carefully on the layout. These lines will outline the motifs on the gouache ground with an indentation line, which will not show when the motifs are painted in gouache. Saral paper, a graphite-backed paper, may be used like carbon paper to transfer the design directly to good paper. This is usually done with designs to be painted in gouache, but should not be used for water-color (the indentations made by direct tracing will show the dry watercolor). Also, since the Saral line sometimes resists the paint, a sample should be tried for the color and technique plan before the transfer of the entire design. Saral line can be erased partially but sometimes not completely. Moving a small piece of Saral paper around causes smudges on the good paper, but Saral can be easily spliced together with transparent tape to yield a piece the size of a large design.

Although dressmaker's carbon paper is more difficult to erase than graphite, it can be used to transfer to colored paper, since it produces a white line rather than the dark line from the graphite paper, which would not show on certain ground papers.

A light table may be used to transfer directly but causes problems similar to the graphite-paper transfer; that is, lines are directly marked on the good paper.

If a design is to be rendered on waxed *masa* paper, the waxed *masa* is placed directly over the polished layout. Because the drawn lines on the layout will be clearly visible, the designer can complete the finished artwork directly on the *masa* paper without transferring the design.

Because many of these methods may have adverse affects on various papers, a small trial should always be made before the entire design is transferred.

After the design is transferred, all plans are made. The artist is ready to render the final artwork.

Using the Computer

Computers can be used to execute any of the steps in the design process. Usually design concepts are developed on paper, generally following the process outlined here, and the computer is used to efficiently manipulate the image and tailor it for implementation into production. This is especially useful in trying more possibilities of colorations in much less time than hand-painting would require.

Rendering Techniques for Printed Designs

5

Once the layout of the textile design has been decided upon, motifs have been carefully drawn, and the layout has been transferred to good paper, two factors remain which are necessary ingredients in the final artwork: the color of the pattern and the rendering technique.

Consummate painting ability, often using gouache and bottled watercolor, is the basis of all textile designing. To fully realize visual ideas on paper, a designer must consistently be able to control these media to produce desired effects.

The most important point to be remembered about techniques in rendering textile designs on paper is that experimentation should never cease. Any method is desirable that can be consistently handled to execute a new, different image in the completed artwork to be reproduced on fabric. These range from popular techniques used in primary-school art courses to practices used by the masters since the Renaissance. A designer should constantly explore all possibilities.

Various painting techniques on paper are standard representations of printing and weaving techniques used in actual fabric manufacture. Even more important, these painting techniques, once mastered, should lead to further experimentation and exploration of design on paper. These innovative painting techniques in turn stimulate new developments in fabric.

However, it must be remembered that, as new media are investigated to better express a designer's ideas, the ultimate product is a piece of fabric. Many interesting techniques on paper have no relation to a textile. A designer must never be confined to how fabric has looked in the past or techniques that have been used in the past. Nevertheless, a pattern is not to be imposed thoughtlessly on a surface; it must be designed as an integral part of fabric, which has characteristics all its own. During planning and execution of artwork on paper, the representation should constantly be thought of in terms of its culmination as fabric.

The most important rule in painting a design is also the simplest: enough paint of each necessary color must be mixed initially to complete the entire painting. The paint can easily be saved in plastic Polycon containers between work sessions;

but if there is not enough paint of a particular color to complete the artwork, it is nearly impossible to remix the exact color, and the slight difference will show in the design. A little forethought will save a lot of aggravation later.

The vast majority of textile designs are painted in a straightforward manner, using either gouache or dye. Gouache is most commonly painted on watercolor paper; dye, on watercolor paper or waxed or unwaxed *masa* paper. But given the numerous types of paper (discussed in the Materials chapter) upon which these media can be used and the many different types of drawing and painting techniques, the variety that can be achieved is endless. Mastery in handling both gouache and dye should be achieved so that almost any desired look can be executed in a relatively simple way, without unnecessary use of complicated painting and rendering techniques.

There are, however, an infinite number of media in which designs can be rendered. The choice is as broad as the designer's imagination.

Gouache

Because such varied effects can be obtained using gouache, it is probably the most commonly used medium in designing for textiles (figures 5–1, 5–2).

Gouache is usually used to paint flat areas of color. With some expertise, a flat, consistent, matte surface can be achieved,

Figure 5–1 *(below left)*
Floral design, flat gouache on paper.
(© *N.J. Cohen*)

Figure 5–2 *(below right)*
Floral design, flat gouache on paper.
(© *Cantoni Satilai*)

yielding the effect of any high-quality printing method executed on opaque fabrics. Gouache is excellent for detailed work because fine points or lines can be painted in one color over another color. It must be remembered that to achieve consistent and detailed work, brushes and gouache must be of the highest quality. Brushes, palettes, and all other materials must be clean and in good condition.

Gouache is mixed by squeezing a small amount of two or three desired colors from the tubes onto the plastic palette. More than three colors blended together tend to become muddy. The colors are thoroughly blended together using a short, stiff-bristled mixing brush. A few drops of clean water are then added from a plastic squeeze-bottle. The mixture should be the consistency of heavy cream.

When a new tube of gouache is opened, an oily, clearish liquid may come out before the paint does. This liquid will hurt the consistency of the paint if mixed in and should therefore be discarded before the paint is extruded.

Blending colors together thoroughly and mixing the paint to the proper viscosity are of primary importance. If colors are not thoroughly blended, the individual colors will appear in streaks when the mixture is painted. Paint that is too thick will drag and not apply evenly, leaving a bumpy and uneven surface. Thick paint also chips more easily. Paint that is too watery will cause translucent streaks to show in the final painting.

With the paint mixed to proper consistency, an area to be painted with gouache should be marked on a piece of paper—perhaps a simple geometric shape. A puddle of gouache should be painted along one edge of the shape, and the paint should then be pulled along quickly, keeping the shape wet until the painting of the shape is completed. The shape should not be outlined with paint and then filled in, for the initial paint lines would show; rather, the body of the brush should be used to fill the whole shape.

Gouache dries quickly, but the paint may appear uneven while it is drying. A second coat should not be applied to gouache. It may change the color slightly, and the surface will not be smooth.

Once painting of some simple shapes is mastered, a simple composition should be drawn and then painted using gouache. A large area should be painted in sections. When it is time to stop painting to refill the brush with paint, the stop should be made in an inconspicuous place, where the overlap of the new and the old paint will be least obvious. During painting, a clear piece of paper should always be placed under the designer's hand to avoid dirtying and smudging of the design while it is in progress.

Gouache can be used on almost any type or color of paper and can also be painted over a gouache surface. Some paint colors are more opaque than others and thus cover the ground more thoroughly. Bleed-proof white paint can opaquely cover a dark surface and can be mixed with other gouache colors to add opacity, although, of course, it will also lighten the color. This property of bleed-proof paint can also be utilized to show lighter values of the same color, represented by fine lines or dots of white painted over an area of another color (figure 5–3).

Dry-brush technique can also be used with gouache to achieve a photographic look. Once shapes are fully painted using the flat technique, one of the darker values of the color is placed on the brush and is allowed to dry for a few seconds; then, around the edges or wherever blending is necessary, this color is brushed lightly over the shapes painted in the lighter value of the color. This technique will be represented by a

Figure 5–3
Floral design, gouache on paper, dots used for shading. (© *Cantoni Satilai*)

separate color when printed; therefore the marks need only be as fine as can actually be reproduced in printing.

Small areas of gouache can be removed from the surface onto which it is applied using one of two methods. The first is to gently scrape away the unwanted paint using a razor blade or X-Acto knife. The second is to wet the area with blotter paper, re-wet with a water-filled brush, and again dry with blotter paper. This process is continued until the area is clean enough to allow the desired changes. These two methods, combined with gouache's ability to cover itself, allow for a tremendous amount of flexibility in this medium.

A gouache surface is extremely fragile and will crack or smudge easily. Erasing pencil marks from a gouache painting causes smudges, although Mars Rasor, handled very gently, works well, with little damage to the paint surface. A painting in gouache should therefore be covered with tracing vellum or acetate for protection and stored carefully.

Bottled Watercolors

Bottled watercolors, which are commonly called dyes, are often used like gouache in a flat technique. Dyes streak very easily and therefore must be manipulated very quickly to

Figure 5–4
Floral design, bottled watercolor on paper, water-color effect used for shading. (© *Cantoni Satilai*)

paint a complete section before any portion of the section dries. Because dye is translucent, corrections cannot be made by repainting over an area. Any mistake with dye will have to be tolerated in the final artwork, but, with practice, dyes can be easily controlled.

Because dyes are translucent, they can be used only on white or off-white papers. These colors are particularly vibrant when painted on translucent papers such as waxed *masa* or tracing vellum. (For the paint to adhere to these surfaces, a few drops of Wax Grip or Noncrawl must be added to it.) This yields a representation of airy, lightweight apparel fabrics; for this reason, dyes are more commonly used to render fabrics in the apparel area than in the decorative.

The translucence of dyes can be used advantageously when one color in the design is painted over another color, yielding a third color. This third color overlap is called a *trap*, or *fall-on*, and represents the same quality that can sometimes be produced on fabric in wet printing methods.

Two or more dye colors can be mixed together, and water can be added to yield lighter values of a color. Since dye color is so intense that one drop will change the color of the mixture greatly, it should be added very sparingly. Dye colors should also be stirred well *each* time the brush is dipped into the paint because the pigment tends to settle to the bottom while the water floats to the top. Likewise, dyes should be shaken well in the bottle each use.

The techniques for painting gouache hold true for dye: a puddle is begun at one side of the shape and pulled along quickly to fill the shape completely. If excess dye is left, it can be removed with a drier brush.

Dye is also commonly used for watercolor techniques (figures 5–4, 5–5), although printing methods that can reproduce shaded effects such as these are limited.

The watercolor technique is executed on paper by using two brushes—one with dye, one with water. The dye is painted along whichever edge of the shape is to be darker. Water is placed along the lighter edge. The water brush is then used to pull the two areas together, blending the values in the middle into a value-graded appearance. This technique can be used for a shaded rendering of a flower, for example.

A watercolor look can also be achieved with dye and bleach (figure 5–6). The design is painted using a flat dye technique on waxed or unwaxed *masa*. Areas that are to be highlighted and lightened are dabbed with a cotton swab that has been soaked in diluted bleach. The bleached area of the painting must then be blotted dry so that excess bleach does not yellow

Figure 5-5
Floral design, bottled watercolor on paper, watercolor effect used for shading. (© *Cantoni Satilai*)

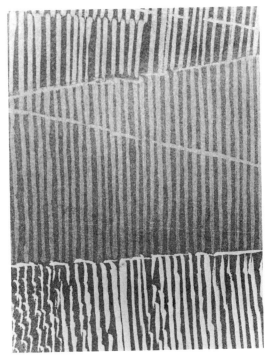

Figure 5-6
Geometric design, bottled watercolor and bleach on paper, bleach used to remove watercolor after it was applied.

on the design. Very soft blending of values can be achieved with this technique. Bleach should never be used with a good brush because it destroys the bristles.

Except that it is often painted on more fragile paper, a dye painting is less fragile than a gouache surface. Dye, however, is not light fast; these designs should be stored with a protected surface.

Painting Grounds and Blotches

A *ground* is a textile surface, dyed or not colored at all, onto which motifs are printed. A background *blotch* area is printed on the fabric in the same manner that the motifs are printed. A ground is most accurately represented on paper either by staining the whole surface before painting the motifs or perhaps by using a colored paper. A blotch is painted after the motifs are painted, and a blotch is almost always painted in gouache, even if the motifs are painted in dye.

A ground is painted with a good-quality, wide varnish or

81

sign cutter's brush. Enough gouache or dye is mixed to cover the entire surface. The surface is then painted quickly using only horizontal strokes. By moving quickly, the designer keeps the paint wet during the entire work time.

Next, the process is repeated with vertical strokes. After this step, the painting is allowed to dry. Gouache may appear to streak while drying, but ultimately it will yield an even surface.

After the surface is dry, the desired technique can be used to execute the motifs.

After the motifs are painted, a blotch is painted using the basic techniques for flat gouache. Again, it is important to keep the blotch paint wet while covering the surface.

To keep the blotch color from being diluted, some artists prefer to dilute black gouache with ink rather than water. If too much ink is added, however, the surface will become shiny.

Markers

One of the simplest and most common techniques is the use of felt- and fiber-tip markers on various papers. Marker on waxed *masa* paper (figure 5–7) yields a look that is similar to that of bottled watercolor on the same paper. Marker on

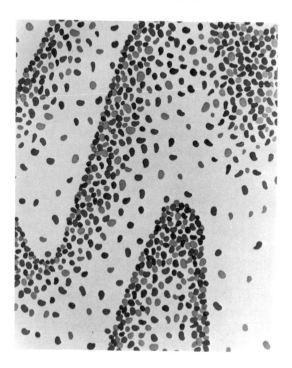

Figure 5–7
Geometric design, marker on *masa* paper. (© N.J. Cohen)

unwaxed *masa* paper makes a soft line. Vellum, plastic-coated papers, and papers sprayed with fixative are all excellent surfaces for marker. The wide variety of colors and points available and the marker's tendency to take on different values and hues on different papers create much versatility in this medium (figure 5–8). The fact that markers, like paint, bleed on some papers must be considered in the planning of designs.

Pen, Ink, and Pencil

The numerous pens and inks that were discussed in the Materials chapter are commonly used in rendering designs. From dip pens with varying points which yield any type of line, to technical (reservoir) pens designed to draw straight lines of consistent width, to dotting pens for small dots, an infinite variety of pens is available, all with specific advantages. Although limitations exist as to which inks can be used with which pens, inks are available in every color as well as metallics (figure 5–9). Through experimentation, every designer learns which tools can be best used to achieve desired results and, conversely, discovers new pens that encourage new design ideas.

Resist Techniques

Several different resist-painting techniques yield interesting effects when interpreted as printed textiles. The most elaborate of these techniques is *batik,* a wax-resist dye method that can be executed on paper in much the same way that it is

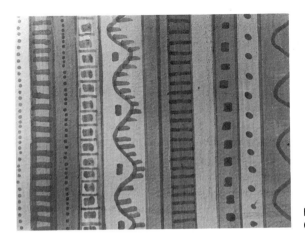

Figure 5–8
Geometric stripe, marker on flat gouache on paper.

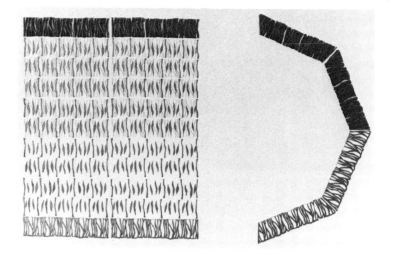

Figure 5-9
Twigs, stripe variations, with octagonal variation for porcelain decoration, ink and gold metallic pigment. (© *1980 Almuth Palinkas, photograph courtesy of the artist*)

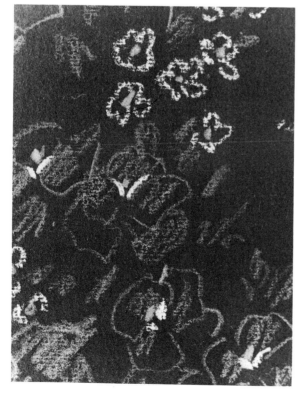

Figure 5-10
Floral, colored pencil on black paper.

Monceau: (above, left) sketchbook, studies, gouache on paper by Corinne Samios; *(above, right)* notebook, study, gouache on paper by Corinne Samios; *(below)* floral documentary (from the Musée des Arts Decoratifs in Paris), print on cotton. (all © Brunschwig & Fils, Inc., photographs courtesy Brunschwig & Fils)

Quel Beau Printemps! bouquet floral, print on cotton. (© Manuel Canovas, Inc., photograph courtesy Manuel Canovas)

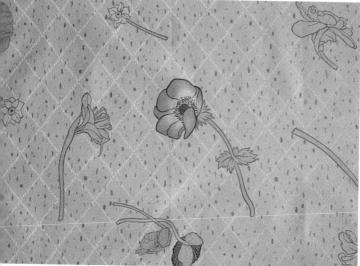

Le Champ Provençal, tossed floral, print on cotton. (© Manuel Canovas, Inc.)

Ginko Leaves, engineered border repeat, ink and dyed on waxed *masa* paper. (© 1983 Almuth Palinkas, photograph courtesy of the artist)

(above) Floral design, gouache on paper (© 1982 Almuth Palinkas, photograph courtesy of the artist); (right) Leaves, engineered border repeat, watercolor on paper. (© 1983 Almuth Palinkas, photograph courtesy of the artist)

Floral, designed by P.C. Turczyn, gouache on paper. (© Crompton Co., photograph Mikio Sekita)

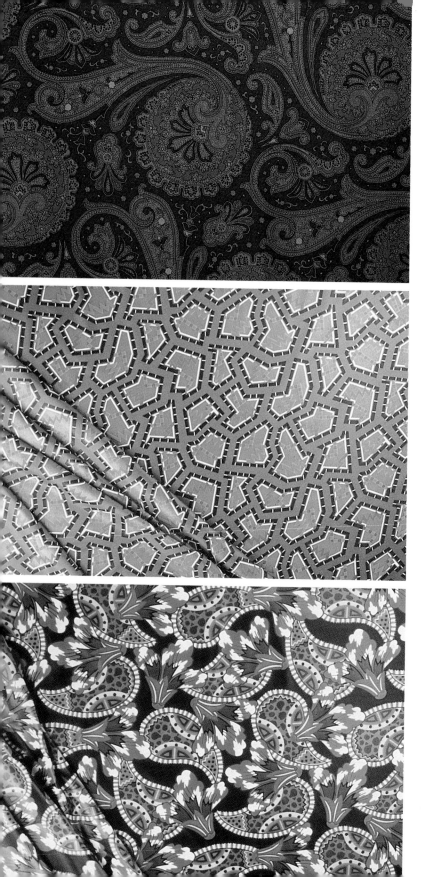

Paisley design, print on silk.
(© Ratti)

Kenya, designed by Nathalie du
Pasquier for Memphis, print on
cotton, produced by Rainbow.
(Photograph courtesy Furniture of
the Twentieth Century, Inc., N.Y.)

Stylized paisley design, printed on
cotton, designed for Memphis,
produced by Rainbow.
(Photograph courtesy Furniture of
the Twentieth Century, Inc., N.Y.)

Champs de Mandarin: (left) original artwork; (below, left) printed cotton; (below, right) printed cotton upholstered on sofa. (© Clarence House, photographs courtesy Clarence House)

Floral, original document.
Collection of Clarence House.
(Photograph courtesy Clarence
House)

Floral, developed from original
document above, print on cotton.
(© Clarence House, photograph
courtesy Clarence House)

(above) Design with birds, gouache on paper (© P.C. Turczyn, photograph Mikio Sekita); (below, left) floral design printed on yarn-dyed ground, rayon/cotton fabric (© Cantoni Satilai); (below, right) color combination of floral design at left. (© Cantoni Satilai)

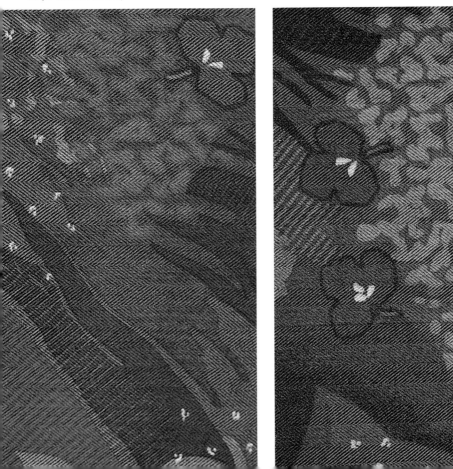

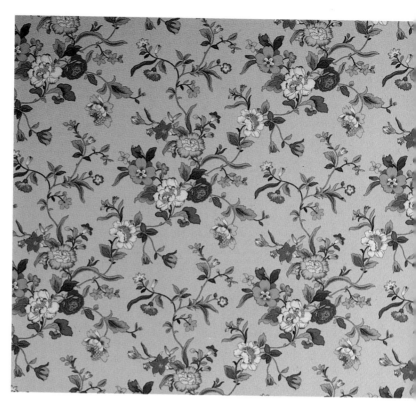

Kayoko, floral design, print on cotton. (© Jay Yang Designs Ltd., photograph courtesy Jay Yang Designs Ltd.)

Parterre, floral design, gouache on paper. (© Brunschwig & Fils, Inc., photograph courtesy Brunschwig & Fils)

Orientalia, floral design, print on cotton. (© Jay Yang Designs Ltd., photograph courtesy Jay Yang Designs)

Paisley design, print on cotton corduroy. (© Cantoni Satilai)

(above) Mira-Columbia, by Verer Panton for Mira-X International Furnishings, Inc., geometric design, print on cotton.

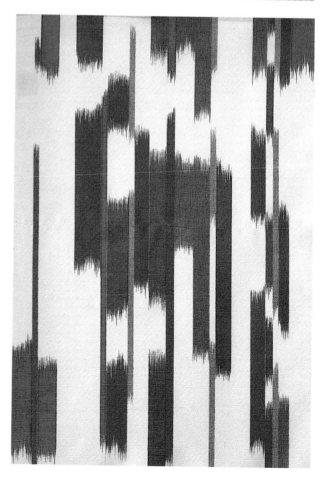

Ikat effect, print on silk. (© Ratti)

Dreamland, abstract design, paint resist technique.
(© Ray Wenzel, photo courtesy Ray Wenzel)

Magic Mountains, all-over abstract texture, with
colorways. (© Ray Wenzel, photo courtesy Ray
Wenzel)

Aquarelle, geometric design with colorways.
(© Ametex/Robert Allen Contract, photo © Scott
Chaney)

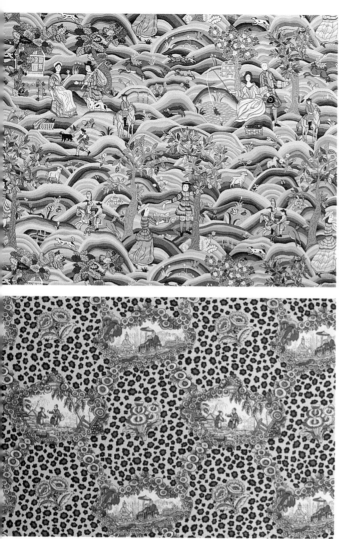

Fishing Lady, conversational design. (© Brunschwig
& Fils, photo courtesy Brunschwig & Fils)

Chinese Leopard Toile, novelty toile design.
(© Brunschwig & Fils, photo courtesy Brunschwig
& Fils)

Matisse, documentary abstract. (© Rodolph Inc.,
photo courtesy Rodolph Inc.)

(above, left) Castille, plaid design with colorways. (© Rodolph Inc., photo courtesy Rodolph Inc.); *(above, right) Imperial Plaid*, plaid design with ikat fill effect. (© Rodolph Inc., photo courtesy Rodolph Inc.); *(below) Samarkand*, bed ensemble. (© The Bibb Company 1994, designer: PC Turczyn, stylist: Gary Filippone, photo courtesy The Bibb Company)

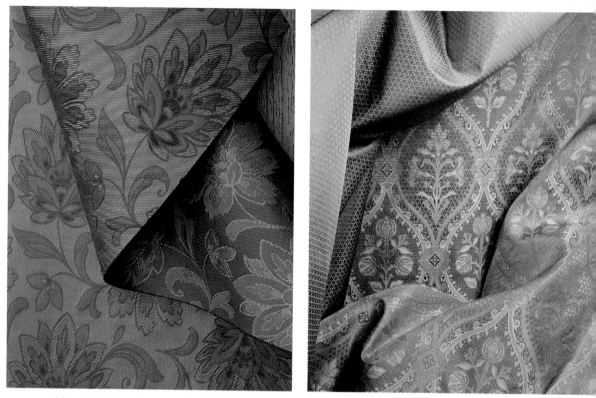

(above, left) Paradise, reversible jacquard floral. (© Pollack & Associates, photo © Maryanne Solensky); *(above, right)* Romance, ogee layout floral, Arts & Crafts–style documentry, and *Flattery*, woven texture. (© Rodolph Inc., photo courtesy Rodolph Inc.); *(below, left)* Wildwood, floral leaf design, and *Network*, geometric design. (© Pollack & Associates, photo © Maryanne Solensky); *(below, right)* Fantasia, ogee layout, fleur-de-lis design and *Sea Field,* jacquard. (© Pollack & Associates, photo © Maryanne Solensky)

Adrian Parry Collection, contemporary designs, prints on cotton. (© Knoll Textiles, photograph courtesy Knoll International)

Floral, three color combinations, gouache on paper. (© N.J. Cohen)

Minton, conversational design, set layout. (© Brunschwig & Fils, photo courtesy Brunschwig & Fils)

(below, left) Coordinated collection of jacquard woven fabrics including *Newport*, frame damask pattern; *Paisley*, paisley pattern; *Roppongi*, abstract texture; and *Coventry*, set design. (© Baker, Knapp and Tubbs, photo courtesy Baker, Knapp and Tubbs); *(below, right) Sultan of Gujarat*, documentary pattern, and Regency chair. (© Brunschwig & Fils, photo courtesy Brunschwig & Fils)

authentically executed on fabric. True batik fabrics are actually impregnated with wax, applied to only certain areas of the cloth to resist color, and some of these batiks are actually on the market; but for more economical production, many batiklike designs are simulated on fabric through screen printing methods rather than by actually waxing the fabric surface. The fabrics are first designed on paper.

The layout for the batik design is very lightly drawn on unwaxed *masa* paper. After the desired colors and shapes are painted using the flat-dye painting technique, the design is allowed to dry. Melted wax (kept hot in the studio with the use of a double boiler on a small hot plate) is then painted over the entire design with a large brush that will henceforth be used only for this purpose, since it is impossible to remove the wax from the bristles afterwards. One edge of the paper should be taped to one edge of the desk and the design held over the air while waxing so that the paper will not stick to any surface.

The waxed paper will cool and harden almost instantly; or it can be rubbed with a cool, wet cloth to speed the process. Once it is cool, the design is carefully crumpled and cracked. The number and density of these cracks are left to the discretion of the designer. It may be done in a random way or in a specific manner to emphasize certain parts of the design. India ink, dye, or even bleach is then rubbed into these cracks. The wax, of course, resists this liquid, but it is absorbed into the original painted surface through the cracks. Bleach will make light-colored fine lines, while ink or dye will directly color the surface.

The excess ink, dye, or bleach must be removed from the waxy surface. The overall appearance can then be inspected and the cracking and coloring redone if desired.

The wax in the paper must then be removed. The design is placed between clean sheets of newsprint. An iron must be applied very briefly so that the wax in the design is melted and transferred to the sheets of newsprint. The process is repeated with the newsprint replaced quickly and often to keep the colors in the design from blending together from the heat. (A sample test should be made before the actual design is ironed.) Likewise, any smudges on the newsprint may be transferred to the design; therefore it is imperative that this paper be perfectly clean before use. All of the wax will not come out of the design paper, but once most of it is removed, the design is complete. Once the wax is applied and removed, the colors that were painted in dye will appear slightly darker than they were when originally painted. Marker can be used on the batik surface to add lines of emphasis or to fill in details.

This process can also be used without marking the paper at all. Simply waxing and ironing out a sheet of unwaxed *masa* paper yields a sheet of waxed *masa* paper, if desired.

A second wax-resist technique is called *tjanting*; again, it is identical to *tjanting* techniques used on fabric.

A *tjanting* (figure 5–11) is a type of "pen" with a wooden handle and a metal spout for a point. Immediately above the spout is a small reservoir cup to hold melted wax, which is applied to a surface through the spout. The point of the *tjanting* is repeatedly dipped into melted wax and then quickly carried to the design paper and used to outline desired shapes. The wax lines serve as boundaries between areas of different colors which can be filled in using bottled water color. Once all the areas of the design are *tjanted* and subsequently colored using bottled dye, the wax must be removed in the same manner that it was removed from the *batik* sheet by ironing the paper.

Around the edges of *tjanting* lines, halos of a darker value of color are left by the spreading of the wax into the surrounding colored area when the paper is heated (figure 5–12). This look may be desired; if not, the entire sheet can be waxed and the wax removed. This will, of course, change all the colors to slightly darker shades because of the application of the wax.

A line similar in character to a *tjanting* line can be achieved on unwaxed *masa* paper, with marker or even by using a plastic squeeze bottle full of paint. These lines will have the characteristic bulb at beginning and end, the same irregular character, and approximately the same size. Using these methods, the line is of course colored, whereas a *tjanting* line resists color and is therefore the natural color of the paper.

Figure 5–11
Tjanting tool.

Figure 5–12
Geometric design, wax (applied with *tjanting*) and bottled watercolor on *masa* paper. (© *N.J. Cohen*)

Simple resist methods which yield different looks are *crayon-resist* and *gouache-resist*.

Crayon-resist can be done in one of two ways. Colored crayons can be used to draw the design, then bottled dye used over the drawing to add a patina or outline the shapes in areas not painted in crayon. White crayon can be used instead, in much the way that the *tjanting* is used, to outline shapes and act as boundaries between areas of different colors to be painted (figure 5–13). Either wax or oil crayons can be used for these techniques. A slightly textured paper works best to give an interesting quality to the edge of the crayon line.

In gouache-resist, small areas of a design are thickly painted in white gouache or poster color. After the gouache is dry, bottled dye is used to color the design as desired. When the entire painting is dry, the gouache is chipped off with a mat or X-Acto knife, exposing paper but leaving a slightly distressed quality to the design.

Similar in concept to a resist, stencils can be used to mask certain areas of the design. It may, at times, be simpler to cut desired shapes from waxed *masa* paper or acetate and, using

87

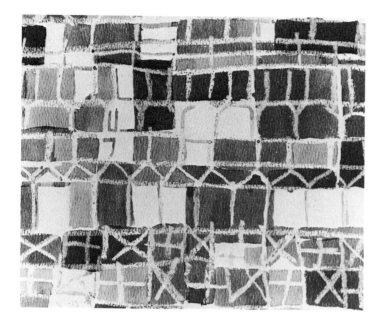

Figure 5–13
Geometric design, crayon resist and
bottled watercolor on paper. (© *1981
Marypaul Yates*)

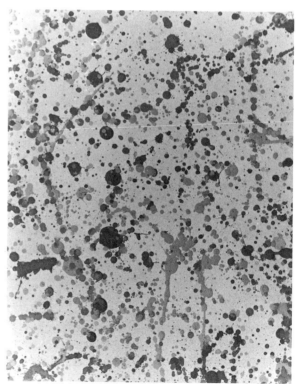

Figure 5–14
Splatter technique, gouache on paper.

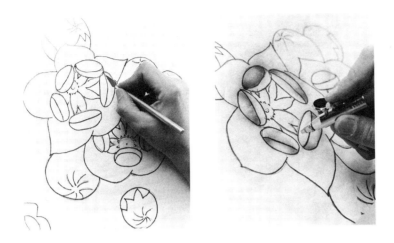

T-pins, attach this stencil over the design, allowing only exposed areas of the paper to be treated with the desired technique (figure 5–14). Stencils are especially useful for messy techniques such as stippling, spraying paint, and air brush, which are most commonly used in painting yarn-dyed plaids. Figures 5–15, 5–16, 5–17, and 5–18 show how an airbrush is used to shade a floral motif.

Liquid maskoid, Frisket, or rubber cement can also be used as a mask. The substance is simply applied to the portion to be masked, the technique executed (figure 5–19) over the rest of the design, and the mask removed.

Different papers with completely different techniques can also be joined together into one design by splicing them. This is covered in the section on Repeats, which is the most com-

Figure 5–15 *(above left)*
Maskit paper (or acetate sprayed with spray adhesive) is placed over the area of the design to be airbrushed. An X-Acto knife is used to cut away the maskit paper from the sections of the motif to be painted in one airbrush color.

Figure 5–16 *(above center)*
The airbrush is used to shade the motif as desired.

Figure 5–17 *(above right)*
All the sections of one color in one area of the pattern are painted at one time.

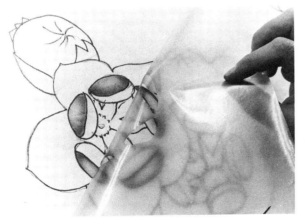

Figure 5–18
Once these sections of the color are dry, the acetate overlay is removed. A new acetate will next be placed over the motif, then the sections to be painted in the next color are unmasked, and the process continued.

Figure 5–19
Floral, stippled gouache on paper.

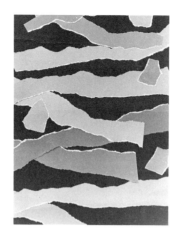

Figure 5–20
Geometric, torn-paper collage.

Figure 5–21
Floral, bottled watercolor on graph paper.

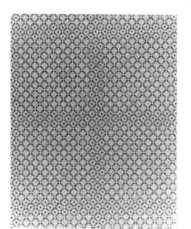

Figure 5–22
Geometric, bottled watercolor on graph paper.

mon application of paper splicing. Interesting effects are obtained through collage techniques (figure 5–20).

Any commonly used artist's material may be used to apply color and line in textile design. Wax and oil crayons have already been mentioned. Pastel is not commonly used because the finished drawing surface is messy and may be destroyed when handled excessively as textile designs often are. Oil paint is not common because it dries so slowly. Acrylic paint is usually considered to be less desirable than gouache for straight painting because it produces a shinier surface, but it can be used for beautiful watercolor techniques and textural surfaces on a design. Any of these materials may be useful in a given situation or on a particular paper.

Surfaces

As previously discussed, innumerable papers in different colors and textures are available, upon which any sort of mark can yield a different look (figures 5–21, 5–22). Gouache designs can be painted on prepared acetate (figures 5–23, 5–24), then superimposed on any desired ground.

Textural qualities may be added to papers to yield results that can be simulated in printing (figures 5–25, 5–26, 5–27). Acrylic paint or thickly applied gouache can be manipulated and embossed for textural grounds.

Scratchboard yields an interesting design ground. Sections of paper are randomly colored in wax crayon, and the entire surface is then painted with black (or any other color) tempera with Wax Grip added. A design can then be scratched through the tempera layer to expose sections of crayon color, which are darkened from the tempera color. The scratchboard surface can be further colored with oil crayons.

Special effects can also be achieved by painting on both sides of translucent papers. Dye on the back of waxed or unwaxed *masa* paper gives a soft ground color. Also, if the technique used on the front of the design is not waterproof, for example, extra marks could be added in dye on the back. Marker could be used for a softer emphasis on the back of a painting.

The multicolored, swirling effect of marbleized paper, long used as book covers, is a popular technique in textile designing (figure 5–28). Different colors of oil-based paint (tube color or enamel paint in cans) are placed side by side on a shallow pan or tray. With a comb the colors are swirled together but not mixed. Once the desired mixture is achieved, the design paper is dipped onto the mixture and thus "printed." This paper is allowed to dry, then used alone, spliced into other techniques, or painted over with other elements. This marbleizing technique is sometimes actually used in production to manufacture wall paper; with fabric, however, the design must be reproduced through screen printing.

Transfer Techniques

Various transfer techniques can be used as collage effects in a design. Rubbings are made by placing rice papers over a relief surface and marking the paper with graphite to pick up the textural quality of whatever is underneath. Magazine,

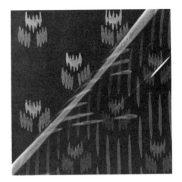

Figure 5–23
Floral, gouache on paper with acetate overlay to show alternate ground treatment. (© *P. Kaufmann, Inc.*)

Figure 5–24 *(above)*
Floral, final version of fig. 5–23 after change in ground. (© *P. Kaufmann, Inc.*)

Figure 5–25
Rome, print on flame retardant polyester featuring texturized ground. (© *Charles Samelson, Inc., American licensee for Pausa*)

Figure 5–26
Geometric gouache on embossed
paper.

Figure 5–27
Floral, gouache on paper using texturizing effect.
(© *Cantoni Satilai*)

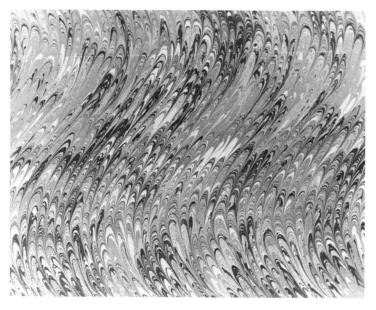

Figure 5–28
Marbleization on paper.

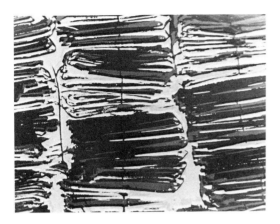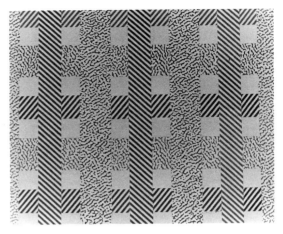

newspaper, or other printed images can be placed over heavy paper, then the printed image soaked in turpentine or lighter fluid. With rubbing, the images will transfer in a slightly distorted way onto the desired paper (figure 5–29). Because turpentine also dissolves oil, oil pastels, and markers, it can be used to manipulate these media. A cloth texture can be imparted to the design surface by placing a piece of cheesecloth over the paper, painting dye over the cloth, and peeling the cloth off the paper. Other images can likewise be transferred to paper.

Wood-block printing is an old method of fabric decoration rarely used in production textiles today, but it yields interesting results on paper that can be simulated on fabric with screen-printing methods. Randomly selected objects, or shapes cut out of a gum eraser, can also be stamped on paper with gouache or dye. This technique can produce a mosaic effect very simply, more easily than by using a brush to paint each small shape individually. Techniques are often devised in this way, not only to achieve a unique look but to save time and annoyance by producing a desired image more easily (figure 5–30).

Figure 5–29 (above left)
New York Times, photomontage.
(© Ann Atkinson)

Figure 5–30 (above right)
Geometric, gouache on paper.

6 Textile-Printing Methods

Several methods are currently used to apply color to textiles to produce pattern, motifs, or designs (figure 6–1). Not all effects can be produced with every one of these printing methods, and the limitations characteristic of each method must be clearly understood by designers wishing to maximize design capabilities.

Roller Printing

In roller printing, a cylindrical copper roller (figure 6–2) is engraved to match exactly the desired textile design. The roller is slightly wider than the fabric to be printed and a maximum of 16″ in circumference. An individual roller is necessary for each color of the desired design; hence, a six-color design is often called a six-roller design. Each roller is etched with the part of the entire motif that it will contribute to the planned design.

Once engraved, each of the necessary rollers is positioned

Figure 6–1 *(below left)*
Printed cotton. (© Lee Jofa, photograph courtesy Lee Jofa)

Figure 6–2 *(below right)*
Engraved copper roller.

Figure 6–3
Roller printing machine.

tangentially to a large drum on the printing machine (figure 6–3). The unprinted fabric is fed into the machine between the drum (which moves the fabric through) and the engraved cylinders (figure 6–4). Below each roller is located a color box containing one color of dye paste and the color is delivered to each roller by an unengraved cylinder (similar to a house-painting roller) called a *color furnisher.* The color furnisher and the engraved roller both spin during printing.

After being mounted on the machine, each engraved roller is adjusted to *register* precisely so that each motif will be exactly located on the fabric. For example, poor registration

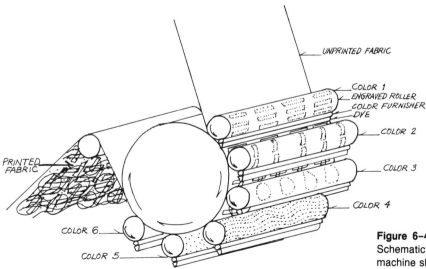

Figure 6–4
Schematic diagram of roller printing machine shown in figure 6–3.

(also called poor *fit*) would result in the edges of a blue flower and a green stem being printed over each other.

Because of the astounding speed of roller printing and the high cost of engraving rollers and setting up the machinery, roller printing is rarely used for fewer than several thousand yards of a particular pattern. Runs of this size almost never occur in home furnishing or contract fabrics; besides, the repeat sizes allowed in roller printing are small for these uses. (Because of the small circumference of the rollers, repeat sizes allowed with this method are limited.) In apparel, however, roller printing is often used; indeed, for long runs roller printing is the most economical printing method.

Once engraved, a copper roller can be used almost indefinitely. However, because apparel patterns do not usually endure on the market for more than a few seasons, the rollers are commonly ground down and re-engraved with a different pattern. Lately this practice has increased due to the rising cost and scarcity of rollers.

In spite of the limitation of small repeat sizes and the necessity of large runs of a single pattern, roller printing allows certain design advantages. Extremely fine, soft lines can be printed with rollers, as in figure 6–5, allowing much detail and subtle, almost photographic, gradation. *Halftones* (shading of light to dark in the same color using only one roller) are, in fact, best achieved with roller printing.

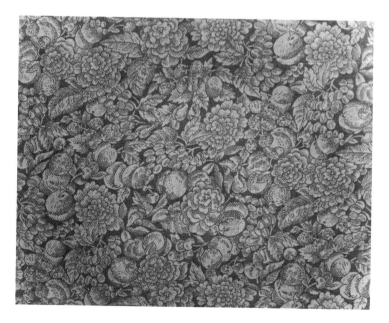

Figure 6–5
Floral, roller print on cotton.
(© *Cantoni Satilai*)

Screen Printing

In screen printing, a finely woven, but open, silk or nylon fabric is mounted over a wooden frame. Depending on the desired design, certain portions of the screen surface are blocked out with an enamel-like covering. The frame is placed in contact with the fabric to be printed; then color is poured into the frame shell and carried back and forth across the screen with a squeegee. The enameled areas of the screen will not allow color to pass through, while the dye paste forced through the unblocked areas of the screen onto the fabric creates the design. As with roller printing, an individual screen for the desired motifs of each color in the complete design is necessary. An eight-color design is therefore referred to as an eight-screen design.

There are three methods of screen printing fabric. In hand and automatic screen printing, the screen is a rectangular frame usually measuring in one direction the width of the goods. In hand screen printing, the fabric is stretched flat on a printing table, the screen is lifted and placed by hand, and the squeegee is operated by hand. In automatic screen printing, the fabric itself is moved along the print table by means of a conveyor belt. As the fabric moves, the screen frames are raised and lowered onto the fabric mechanically (figures 6–6, 6–7). When the frame is lowered into position for printing,

Figure 6–6
Flat-bed screen printing.

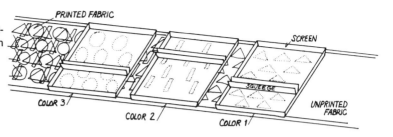

Figure 6–7
Schematic diagram of automatic flat-bed screen printing machine shown in figure 6–6.

PRINTED FABRIC

SCREEN

SQUEEGE

COLOR 3

COLOR 2

COLOR 1

UNPRINTED FABRIC

the squeegee carries the dye paste across the frame automatically.

Automatic flat-bed screen printing is a relatively slow and expensive method of printing. It is, however, in common use for small runs of fabric (fewer than 2,000 yards of a particular pattern), and allows very large repeat sizes. Engineered patterns must be printed with flat-bed printing because of the repeat sizes required.

Hand screen printing is rarely used in production quantities. Because of the expense involved, it is used only by certain custom or very small specialty printers.

Rotary screen printing (figures 6–8, 6–9, 6–10), the fastest method of screen printing, is used for quantities of fabric somewhat smaller than those for roller printing. In rotary printing, as in automatic flat-bed printing, the fabric moves along a table or conveyor. The screens, made of fine aluminum

Figure 6–8
Rotary screen printing.

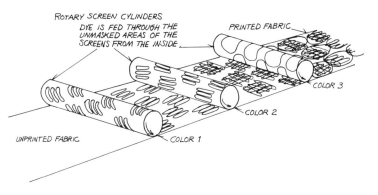

ROTARY SCREEN CYLINDERS
DYE IS FED THROUGH THE
UNMASKED AREAS OF THE
SCREENS FROM THE INSIDE

PRINTED FABRIC

COLOR 3

COLOR 2

UNPRINTED FABRIC

COLOR 1

Figure 6–9
Schematic diagram of rotary printing machine shown in figure 6–8.

mesh, are cylindrical (figure 6–11), and as the cylinder turns and the fabric moves along, dye is applied onto the fabric from the inside through the unblocked areas of the cylinder's surface. Again, because each cylinder delivers one color to the fabric, as many rotary screens are necessary as there are colors in the design. Rotary printing allows repeat sizes larger than those of roller printing but smaller than flat-bed screens. It is extremely accurate in registration.

Because the fabric is continuously printed, warp-way stripes are most commonly printed using rotary screens. These stripes could not be easily side-matched in flat-bed screen printing each time the screens had to be repositioned.

Screen print patterns are often of bold, simple shapes. In flat-bed printing, the dye dries slightly between each screen, producing a crisper, cleaner look and finer line than in rotary printing, where each color is applied to the cloth continuously. This characteristic must be compensated for in design: since

Figure 6–10 *(below left)*
Rotary screen printing.

Figure 6–11 *(below right)*
Rotary screens.

the colors will become more similar to one another during the printing process, more contrasting colors than actually desired must be requested. Consequently, fine detail is much more easily achieved in flat-bed than in rotary printing. However, more detail can be achieved by using a finer mesh screen, the limitation being that the denser the screen, the more likely the dye paste will clog during printing. True halftones are not possible in screen printing but are simulated with dots of a particular color closely or distantly spaced, an effect called *bendé* (figure 6–12). Even this technique can be successfully used in very small areas only.

Fall-on effects, in which two colors overlap to result in a third color, are best achieved with flat-bed printing, again because the first color is allowed to dry slightly before the second color is applied. Because dyes may resist each other or react unpredictably when mixed together (this is true even on paper when one color of bottled watercolor is painted over another), fall-ons are not often used. If a third color is absolutely necessary, an additional screen would probably best be used to provide it. In rotary printing, the fine-mesh Penta screens allow greater line detail; and Galvanos screens, which are made of nickel and which are built up themselves to block the desired areas, are used for shaded effects.

In most instances, the advantages of rotary printing outweigh its disadvantages; it is therefore the most popular printing method in the fabric industry today.

Figure 6–12
The design on the left is painted in dye using a watercolor effect. The right side shows the same design adapted into flat areas of gouache color so that it can be screen printed.

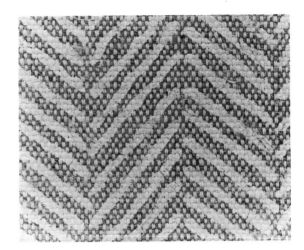

Figure 6-13
Geometric, pigment white printed on linen ground.
(© *Hinson & Co.*)

Dry Printing

In roller and screen printing the type of dye used and the method of its application affect the detail of design that can be achieved.

In dry printing, the cloth to be printed is dry, and pigments, which are not actually dyes, are applied to the cloth. Because the pigment does not interact with the fabric but sits on its surface, bound with resin binders, a stiffness (and sometimes a noticeable thickness) is produced where the color is applied. Although they have good fastness to light, the colors are not particularly fast to water or *crocking* (abrasion). Special effects can be achieved by this building onto the fabric surface, and pigment white is especially common as a design effect (figure 6-13). Metallic and pearlescent pigments, likewise, have come into popular use. In drapery and curtain fabrics, which will receive little abrasion and be dry cleaned and not laundered, pigment printing is common. Compared with dyed fabrics, dry-printed fabrics require little processing after being printed.

Wet Printing

Direct wet printing is most common. In this method, the cloth is damp and is impregnated with dyes that chemically bond with the surface of the cloth. The dye *class* used depends on the type of fiber to be printed. For example, *vat* dyes bond with cellulosic fibers and *disperse* dyes with synthetics. After printing, the dyes are heat set, and the fabric is washed and dried. In direct printing, the color is applied directly onto a white cloth with one of the methods previously described. If

101

the cloth has been previously dyed a color other than white, the applied colors will become darker as they combine with the *ground* color. If desired, the background area may be printed in the same manner as the motifs. This is called *blotch* printing: the printed background area is called a blotch. The blotch usually is made to overlap edges of all motifs by a fraction of an inch so that no lines of the fabric underneath show. Such lines, indicating that the blotch did not *fit* properly, are called *grins.*

Discharge Printing

In some cases, instead of a dark ground color being printed as a blotch, the entire cloth is piece-dyed to the desired shade before the fabric is printed. If the dyed fabric were then printed over, the colors would be quite distorted by the underlying dark color; therefore, a substance containing a bleaching agent as well as a dye paste is applied to the cloth. The dark dye is thereby removed from specified areas of the cloth, which is then immediately impregnated with the new dye color as desired. Because it requires the extra piece-dye process, *discharge printing* is expensive, but it achieves complete coverage of large, colored ground areas. Almost exclusively used for apparel fabrics, discharge prints can be recognized not only by solid ground area on both the front and back of the goods, but also by slight halos around the motifs (figure 6–14).

Figure 6–14
Floral, discharge print on silk. (Note halos around edges of motifs.)

Figure 6-15
Processing of printed fabrics in the print plant.

Other Printing Methods

In *burn-out printing,* which is similar to discharge printing, a bleaching agent (or acid) is applied to the cloth. This substance literally removes portions of the fabric, leaving translucent spots. The fabrics are usually of a polyester ground with a supplementary weft of rayon or cotton. The acid removes the cellulosic fiber and leaves the polyester.

Flock prints are made by applying an adhesive to the ground cloth in certain areas and then dusting the fabric with fine, loose fibers. The fabric is similar in appearance to a patterned velvet.

In *warp printing,* the warp is printed or resist-dyed before the fabric is woven. When the fabric is woven, the warp yarns shift slightly, and hazy, broken-edged motifs are produced. This technique, which originated in France in the eighteenth century, produces a fabric called *chiné. Ikat,* which originated in Indonesia, and Japanese *kasuri* techniques yield a similar appearance with a resist-dyed (rather than direct-printed) warp. The motifs and types of patterns in these fabrics differ, but the term *ikat* popularly refers to warp-printed or warp-resist-dyed fabrics of any origin. These techniques are very expensive and rarely done in production quantities, but the effects are often simulated in printed patterns.

Heat-Transfer Printing

Completely different from roller and screen printing, *heat-transfer,* or *sublistatic,* printing is executed by first printing the design on paper, with inks containing disperse dyes. The

103

Figure 6-16
Schematic diagram of heat-transfer printing machine.

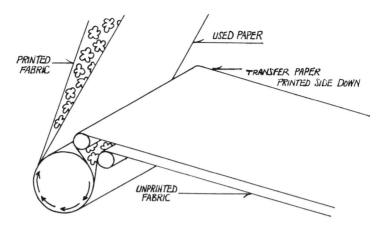

PRINTED FABRIC

USED PAPER

TRANSFER PAPER
PRINTED SIDE DOWN

UNPRINTED FABRIC

printed paper is then pressed together with the fabric through a heat-transfer machine. Under high temperatures the dye *sublimates* (changes from solid to gas) and transfers onto the fabric (figure 6–16). Disperse dyes are the only class that can be used; since only certain synthetics have an affinity for these dyes, heat-transfer printing is possible only on synthetic fabrics. Printing of the transfer paper requires long lead time and large minimum yardages, but the transfer can be made to fabric quickly with relatively inexpensive, compact equipment.

Heat-transfer printing is less widely used than other methods. Although any number of colors can be used and photographic and watercolor effects can be accurately replicated, heat-transfer-printed colors are somewhat lacking in intensity and depth, and the prints tend to have a decal-like appearance. Pictorial scenes and realistically rendered florals are common heat-transfer products.

The Process of Designing Woven Fabric

7

The preceding chapters have emphasized practices in designing patterns to be printed onto a fabric. The fabric itself may be woven, knitted, or, in limited instances, tufted or nonwoven. Woven fabrics are by far the most common print base: they are the usual fabric structure for apparel or household end uses.

While some woven fabrics are used solely as cloth to print onto, others are developed to be dyed as solid colors, or are woven as stripes, plaids, or patterns. Some designers specialize in woven design, but print designers also often handle some aspects of woven design as a part of their jobs.

Design of woven fabric in industry is accomplished in a variety of ways, depending largely on the type of woven fabric. A successful, innovative designer needs extensive knowledge of weaving and other methods of fabric production, and excellent references are available on this extensive subject.* This text emphasizes design practices in industry for various types of woven textiles, and while technical aspects of fabric construction are discussed minimally, basic terminology is defined as it relates to these design practices.

Woven fabrics (which are intended to be used as such, not to be printed over) are usually colored in one of two ways, either by *piece-dyeing* or by *yarn-dyeing.* In the first case, the fabric is woven of yarn in a natural, or undyed, state and large amounts of the fabric are dyed after being woven. This fabric is called piece-dyed, because the bolts of fabric, called pieces, are dyed together. If diverse fibers make up the cloth, they are usually dyed to the same color, although each fiber may require a different type, or *class,* of dye. This process, called *union-dyeing,* produces a fabric of a solid color.

Fabric made of different fibers that accept different classes of dye may be piece-dyed by only one dye class so that one of the fibers remains undyed; or, in fact, each fiber within one

---

*Some of the widely used books on woven design are Allen Fannin's *Handloom Weaving Technology,* Mary Kirby's *Designing on the Loom,* G. H. Oelsner's *A Handbook of Weaves,* Pierre Ryall's *Weaving Techniques for the Multiple Harness Loom,* and W. Watson's *Textile Design and Color* and *Advanced Textile Design.*

cloth may be dyed to a different color. The technology for this process, called *cross-dyeing,* is not commercially practical for use with more than two different dye classes.

Piece-dyed fabrics are usually constructed of basic weaves (plain weaves, twill, or satin) or simple dobby weaves (small, geometric patterns produced by a multi-harness loom). Design of these fabrics includes development of extensive *color lines*—the solid colors that will be dyed for each cloth. A designer chooses the group of these colors and usually sends swatches of the desired color to a dyer who makes small trials called *lab dips* before the final decisions are made.

More importantly, a designer of piece-dyed fabrics guides the textile company in the development of new fabric constructions that are appropriate for weight, hand, look, and price point. This involves development of new yarns as well as ways that yarns, weaves, and finishing techniques can be used together to yield a new cloth. In conjunction with technical personnel, a designer's importance in this role cannot be underestimated. It is difficult to arrive at a new, successful solid fabric; but once such a cloth is developed, it usually remains on the market for many years and is financially important for the textile company. Most often, developmental trials for new piece-dyed fabrics are made in actual production, by the mill developing the fabric according to written instructions from the mill's developmental staff.

The other major category of nonprinted fabrics is produced from yarns that are already dyed before the fabric is made. Although, when woven, these yarn-dyed fabrics may require some finishing process, the fabric is already completely colored. Usually no other color is applied to the cloth, although occasionally a yarn-dyed cloth is overprinted or overdyed.

A textile is, literally, a fabric produced by weaving. Woven fabrics are constructed by interlacing two sets of threads at right angles to each other. The vertical set is called the *warp,* and the horizontal is called the *weft* (or filling). An individual warp thread is an *end;* an individual filling thread is a *pick.*

If one of these sets of threads is a solid color and the other set varies in color, a stripe results. Bands of color in both warp and filling directions produce a plaid or checked fabric. Although often simulated in printed fabrics, stripes and plaids make up the majority of yarn-dyed fabric constructions.

Computer-generated artwork is increasingly used to create yarn-dyed patterns (see page 132). Yarn-dyed patterns are usually designed in one of two ways. In the first method, stripes and plaids of various styles, patterns, and proportions are tried in samples that are actually woven on hand-looms, or at the mill in production. In the second method, an accurate painting of the intended design is made on paper before a sample is ever woven. As with prints, once certain patterns are chosen, various color looks for each pattern are developed later.

Whether samples are woven on a hand-loom or at the mill on a power loom depends largely on the structure of the specific organization. It is probably most advantageous for the first trial to be made on a power loom: it is much quicker, and potential manufacturing problems can often be eliminated at this initial stage. However, some mills are not equipped to handle large quantities of sample weaving at the mill; therefore, some initial screening of samples must be done on a hand-sample basis. As a general rule, converters who work with several mills weave most of their samples on hand-looms, while large upholstery mills weave samples at the mill.

Although apparel yarn-dyes may be handled in either of these ways, they are also commonly designed as paintings on paper before the fabric samples are made. While these paintings are startlingly realistic renditions of woven fabrics, they cannot accurately depict differences in yarn types and elaborate weave structures. Therefore, these paintings are most commonly used for *fine count* (a large number of threads per inch of fabric) and *balanced* cloths (an approximately equal number of threads in both vertical and horizontal directions), such as shirtings, tartan-like plaids, and smooth suiting fabrics.

Types of Yarn-Dyed Designs

Like printed fabrics, yarn-dye patterns fall into several broad categories. As previously mentioned, a stripe is a woven fabric in which all threads in one direction are the same color and the threads in the other direction are of different colors. The stripe may run in either the warp or filling direction. In a plaid fabric there is more than one color used in both the warp (vertical) and filling (horizontal) direction.

A *balanced stripe* essentially means a symmetrical layout: the configuration of colored bands has a "center," and going out from that axis there are idential corresponding bands on either side of the center (figure 7–1). An *unbalanced* stripe is any other type of layout; that is, an asymmetrical stripe (figure 7–2).

A *two-dimensional, three-dimensional,* etc., pattern refers to the number of different sizes of stripes within the pattern. A pattern may have four different colors of stripes but only two

107

different widths of these colored bands in the pattern; thus it is a two-dimensional stripe.

A *striae* (pronounced 'strī-ē) is a stripe that changes subtly in color and/or texture throughout the fabric, almost like a slightly variegated solid (figure 7–3). There are no strong breaks in color in a striae as there are in most stripes; but like a stripe, a striae is made by careful mixing of bands of color in only one direction.

An *ombre* (pronounced 'äm-brā) is composed of distinct bands of color which are closely related in hue, value, or intensity, placed in graded order from darkest to lightest, or dullest to brightest (figure 7–4). Also, an ombre could show bands, for example, starting with blue, continuing through

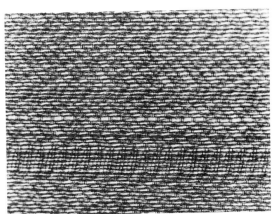

Figure 7–3 *(left)*
Striae (variegated effect), rayon/silk fabric. (© *American Silk Mills Corp.*)

Figure 7–4 *(above)*
The sections of this stripe, between the large, dark bands are *ombre* effects. Satin stripe, gouache on paper.

blue-green, then green-blue, then green, and back the other way to blue. The stripes of an ombre usually have an equal difference in value between every two adjacent stripes, without a noticeable jump greater than any other jump.

Satin stripes are often mixed with other weaves to change color and texture. In a *satin weave,* almost all of the warp (or filling) threads float on the surface. Because the threads in the other direction hardly show on the surface of a satin weave, a shinier face with richer color is produced (figure 7–5). Stripes of satin weave, or another weave, are often mixed into the ground of a basic weave. Figure 7–6 shows a plaid composed

Figure 7–5 *(left)*
Plaid (above) with satin-stripe coordinate (below), gouache on paper. (© *N.J. Cohen*)

Figure 7–6 *(below)*
Plaid with dobby weave effects, cotton/wool fabric. (© *American Silk Mills Corp.*)

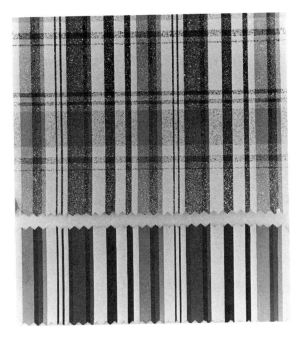

of several different weave effects used in the colored warp stripes.

A *true* design has the identical stripe in the warp and fillings; therefore it is a plaid that looks the same vertically and horizontally (figure 7–7). In a *mongrel* design the layout of the warp and filling stripes differ. Mongrel designs are more common than true designs; in production, warp stripes, once set, are rarely changed; yet with little extra effort, filling patterns can be changed constantly. Looms are mechanically limited to a maximum number of colors in the filling (weft) direction, but the warp can be set up with as many colors as the mill is willing to use. For this reason a warp stripe may be established with many colors and crossed with different filling stripes to yield different patterns. The filling stripes may, in some instances, accommodate only four colors.

A *tartan,* literally, is a worsted or woolen cloth woven as a plaid and worn chiefly by Scottish highlanders, each clan having its own distinctive design called by the name of the clan. In looser terminology, tartans are any plaids of the bold reds, blues, greens, and yellows with black-and-white accents, in balanced (sometimes true) designs, usually woven in the twill or plain weave typical of Scottish tartans. Because they are so commonly used in fall children's clothing, tartans are sometimes called "back-to-school plaids."

An *end-and-end* design signifies a stripe or plaid in which every other warp thread alternates in a contrasting color— perhaps black, white, black, white. When this end-and-end stripe is crossed with a solid filling, a tiny pinpointing of color results because the filling is closer in hue and value to one of the warp colors than to the other. An end-and-end pattern (or,

Figure 7–7
True design, gouache on paper. (© *N.J. Cohen*)

similarly, a pick-and-pick design, in which filling threads alternate in color) yields a unique effect because of the fine mix of the contrasting colors in separate yarns. Certain looms are equipped to weave pick-and-pick designs; other (mostly older) looms are not capable of weaving these effects. End-and-end patterns can be woven by any mill that is willing to make a warp of this arrangement.

A *menswear* design signifies any stripe or plaid done in the neat, fine, usually conservative proportions and colors of men's suiting or shirting.

Gingham checks are true, one-dimensional designs (figure 7–8). The warp and filling stripes are identical, with equal stripes alternating between white and a color.

Any stripe or plaid can contain a variegated or *space-dyed* yarn—that is, a single yarn that changes color within one length of the yarn. Before it is woven, yarn is space-dyed by special processes that inject dye into the yarn at alternating intervals. *Variegated* yarn is made by spinning together different colors of fiber to produce a single yarn. Heather effects are achieved in one of these two ways.

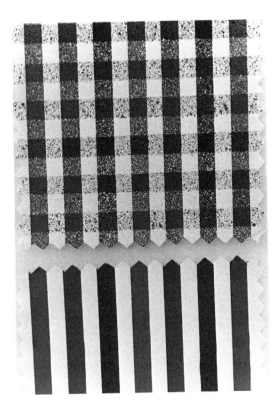

Figure 7–8
Gingham check (*above*) with satin-stripe coordinate (*below*), gouache on paper. (© *N.J. Cohen*)

Iridescent fabrics are produced most successfully in balanced fabrics, usually of fine count. The warp is a solid color, and the filling is a different solid color. The different warp and filling colors must be either very close, adjacent colors or complementary colors (opposites on the color wheel). Either of these methods will produce a fabric that is almost solid in appearance but changes color slightly when the fabric is viewed from different angles.

Like prints, yarn-dyed fabrics are commonly designed as coordinate groups. A plaid may coordinate with the same warp stripe using a solid filling. Gingham checks of the same colors but different scales may be used together. A plaid may even be designed in similar color and scale to coordinate with a print. It is, however, impossible to reproduce a color identically in yarn-dyed, printed, and piece-dyed fabrics. Even if the identical color exists, it will look different when applied to the fabric by different dyeing methods.

Painting the Yarn-Dyed Design

As previously described, these stripes and plaids may be designed as woven samples either at the mill or on hand-looms. If, however, they are designed on paper beforehand, very specific methods are used to render these designs.

Like all fabric designs, yarn-dyed designs are begun with rough sketches. Because the relative translucence of both approximates how warp and filling threads will look when crossed in weaving, colored pencil or bottled watercolor are excellent media for these sketches. Maximum numbers of colors in warp and filling direction depend entirely on the mill that will manufacture the fabric and the type of loom on which it will be woven.

Drawing the Layout

For simplicity, this description outlines the process used by right-handed designers. Left-handed artists would work from the upper right corner axis to avoid problems of wet paint while working. In that case, left-right orientations that are used here should be reversed.

To begin the polished layout, the designer sets up a small drawing board on which an 11"x 14"piece of kid-finish Bristol board is centered, the full length of all four sides attached by narrow masking tape to the board. The longer sides of the drawing board and the paper should be horizontal (figure 7–9).

Figure 7–9
The paper is attached to the drawing board, and the pencil markings are made to show the warp layout of the plaid to be painted.

A T-square with beveled edges is then placed horizontally across the paper. Using the T-square and pencil, the artist marks the top edge of the design about an inch from the top edge of the paper and along the long edge of the paper. The designer similarly marks the left edge of the design, placing the T-square vertically, again penciling a line extending down the paper approximately an inch from its left edge.

The desired warp pattern will be painted horizontally and the filling arrangement vertically. This is the opposite of the way the fabric will be woven.

Beginning about an inch below the upper pencil boundary, the artist measures intervals for the desired warp-stripe proportions, marking in the margin along the left-hand pencil edge of the design. For example, a ½" stripe may be followed by two 1" stripes, a ¼" stripe, and a ⅛" stripe, and then mirrored back: ¼", two 1", and ½". Three entire repeats of the desired arrangement should be marked along the left pencil boundary. It is essential that these measurements be absolutely accurate; a hairline difference in the measurement will show as a vast error when the line is extended across the design.

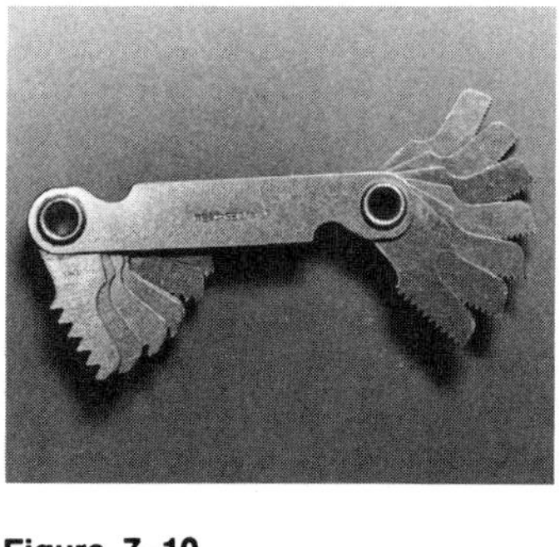

A tool called a *screw-pitch gauge* (figure 7–10), available at hardware stores, can be used to measure small-width stripes. This small metal tool features several combs, each with a specific number of teeth per inch. The teeth can be stamped

Figure 7–10
Screw-pitch gauge.

onto an ink pad and then onto the design paper to measure off even units of desired small intervals. This is a much quicker and more accurate way to measure the numerous intricate spaces required in many yarn-dyed designs.

Next, beginning about an inch to the right of the left pencil boundary, the proportions of the filling stripes are similarly marked across the top pencil edge of the design. Again, three repeats of the design are necessary, and the lines are marked only in the top margin.

Painting the Warp

The warp is painted in gouache with a ruling pen and a good sable brush. Initially, as with any design, enough paint of each desired color must be mixed to complete the entire design.

Next, all stripes in the warp of the *lightest* color to be used are painted. Because these stripes will next be bordered by stripes of other colors, it is not important that they be confined to their proposed boundaries; rather, they should slightly overflow into the next stripe on either side (figure 7–11).

The gouache must be mixed to the proper consistency. Once this is done, the entire length of the stripe is painted in a long sweeping motion in one stroke. The stroke should begin a little to the right of the left pencil boundary but not close enough to cover the markings in the margin. (The finished design will later be cropped to the desired size.)

Figure 7–11
When a stripe is painted between two stripes that have not yet been painted (working from light to dark colors), the brush overflows into the two adjacent stripes.

To help keep the brush moving in a straight line, the artist should place an engineer's scale along the bottom boundary of the stripe to be painted. The scale is then tilted toward the artist so that only one edge rests on the paper and the scale is parallel to the stripe. The brush can then be rested against the scale and moved along to follow the stripe.

All of the other lightest-color stripes are then painted in a similar manner, starting with the top one and working down the design to the bottom. In this manner, no unnecessary time is spent waiting for paint to dry, and neither the T-square nor the designer's hand are placed in wet paint.

The second-lightest-color stripes are painted next. Where these stripes border yet unpainted sections, this second set of stripes may be painted in the same manner as the first.

Where these stripes border the already painted lighter-color stripes, the ruling pen must be used. In this case, the T-square is placed exactly on the marking that signifies the edge of the stripe: it rests along the line to be painted. Again, care is taken to preserve accuracy. This line need not be marked in pencil since the pencil line sometimes resists gouache.

The prongs of the ruling pen are adjusted to approximately 1/16″ apart so that the pen both holds enough paint to complete a line the length of the page and allows paint to flow easily (figure 7–12). Each time new paint is used, trials should be made to assure its proper adjustment before the actual design is painted.

Once the ruling pen and paint are ready, the pen is used in the same manner in which the brush was used: one long stroke, beginning just to the right of the left pencil margin, continues across the entire length of the paper (figure 7–13).

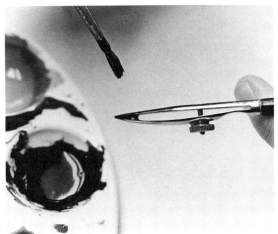

Figure 7–12
Gouache is placed in the ruling pen.

The ruling pen must always be held with the flat edge towards the designer, at a consistent 45° angle to the paper.

Only when the stripe or stripes that border it have already been painted is the ruling pen used to draw the edge of the stripe (figure 7–14). If the stripe on one side has been painted but the other side has not, the ruling pen is used to draw the line against the painted stripe, and the brush is used to fill in the stripe. In this case the brush stroke must meet the ruling pen line exactly, but it should overflow into the adjacent stripe on the other side, which has not been painted (figure 7–15). If

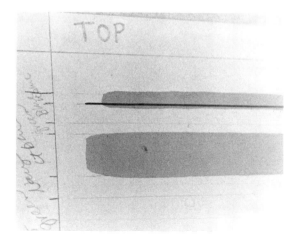

Figure 7–14
Two stripes have already been painted using only a brush. These stripes were painted to overflow into the adjacent stripes. The ruling pen line was then drawn along an edge where a darker stripe will border on the already painted stripe.

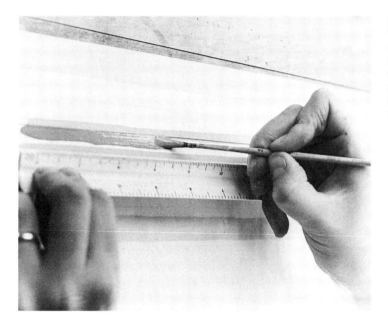

Figure 7–15
The darker stripe is painted, on the upper edge to exactly meet the ruling pen line, and on the lower edge to overflow into the adjacent, not yet painted stripe. An engineer's rule serves as a guide to brace the artist's hand.

the bordering stripes on both sides have already been painted, the ruling pen is used to draw both edges of the new stripe (figure 7–16), and the brush is used to fill in the stripe, keeping the stroke exactly between the two ruling pen border-lines (figure 7–17).

The brush stroke that completes the stripe (between the ruling pen lines) must be executed as one smooth, continuous stroke. If the stripe is painted over more than once, the surface of the painting will not be smooth and consistent. With practice, it is easy to execute this "perfect" stroke. Obviously, all

Figure 7–16
Two ruling pen boundary lines are drawn where a new stripe meets adjacent already painted stripes on both sides.

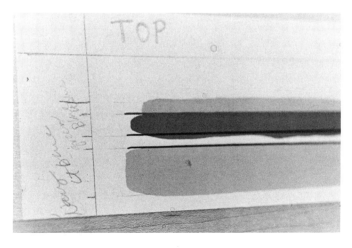

Figure 7–17
A brush is used to paint the final
stroke between the two ruling pen
lines shown in fig. 7–16.

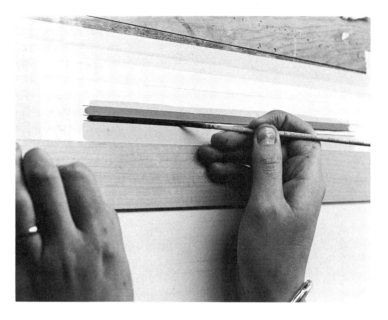

of these techniques should be practiced before a complete design is attempted.

The entire warp is painted in this manner, using brush and ruling pen. Care must also be taken to lift the T-square precisely each time that it is moved. If the T-square is pushed across the design, the paint will smudge and destroy the straightedge painted lines. As always, to avoid dirtying and smudging the design, a piece of paper should be placed under the designer's hand during the painting process.

Stippling the Filling

Once the warp is complete, the filling stripes, which run from top to bottom on the paper, are painted with a stippling or airbrush technique.

Because of the ease, speed, and consistency with which it produces the desired effect, either a studio or an individual designer working with any regularity on these yarn-dyed designs will probably purchase an airbrush. However, stippling with toothbrushes quite adequately produces the proper look.

Because these techniques are messy, at each stage the entire design except for the section being painted must be masked. Likewise, any other paper, artwork, or materials near the work space should be covered.

Again, the lightest-color stripes are painted first. Two *clean*

118

sheets of white paper are placed on the design, one covering everything to the left of the stripe to be painted, the other covering everything to the right of the stripe (figure 7–18). So that even the bordering stripes are well covered, the papers must be placed exactly on the edges of the stripe. Each sheet of paper is then weighted with a thin steel bar a bit longer than the stripe being painted. These bars, which resemble very heavy, bulky metal rulers (with no markings, of course), are available from scrap-metal shops. Each bar is placed on the sheet of clean paper about 1/16″ away from the edge of the stripe to be painted and in the direction of the stripe.

The filling stripe is then stippled. A paint brush is used to deposit two or three drops of the desired gouache color on a good-quality natural-bristle toothbrush. Holding the brush bristle-side down over the design, the artist runs a sharp knife across the bristles to splatter the paint over the stripe. Practice and excellent materials—gouache at a buttermilk-like consistency, a new stiff toothbrush, a sharp knife—will produce fine, even dots instead of irregular splatter.

This "stippling" technique is continued over the stripe to produce an even covering. As previously stated, an airbrush is the best tool for this effect and should be used if available. The same consistent, even surface should be produced in this case, but it is largely dependent on the quality and condition of the airbrush being used.

If toothbrushes are used, it is a good idea to keep four to six on hand and to use each exclusively for one color. For example, one brush can be labeled for white/off white only, one for yellow, one for red, one for navy or black. Although they can be cleaned, some residue of color may hold.

Once the stippled stripe is *completely* dry, the paper and metal bars are lifted and replaced on the next stripe. Again, as with the warp stripes, the stripes of the lightest color should be painted first, the next lightest second, and so on. Also, the paper and metal bars must not be pushed across the surface of the painting; they must be lifted carefully each time they are moved.

Once this entire process is completed and all the filling stripes are stippled, the painting is complete. The paper is removed from the board, and the rough edges with measuring and miscellaneous markings are cropped. As actual fabric samples would be, the edges of these designs are commonly cut with pinking shears.

An alternate method is often used to mask the painting during the filling-stripe stippling. A sheet of Frisket paper (or a sheet of acetate lightly misted on one side with spray adhe-

Figure 7–18
After the warp is painted and is completely dry, paper is placed over the painting so that only one filling stripe is exposed. The paper for masking is weighted using metal bars. The exposed filling stripe is then stippled with the desired color.

119

sive) is affixed to the warp stripe that is already painted. The adhesive paper may first be pressed onto another surface to remove excess stickiness and then placed on the painting. Using a T-square and an X-Acto knife, sections of the acetate are scored but not cut all the way through. These sections are then peeled away so that all of the stripes of one desired filling color are exposed. The exposed stripes are then stippled, and after they are dry, the remaining acetate is removed. The process is repeated as needed for each different color of filling stripe. This method is needed to attain accuracy. Placing and replacing the metal bars for each stripe can be tedious, time consuming, and much less precise.

Techniques for Painting Other Effects

Various weaves and special yarn effects are painted in specific ways. In a satin weave the warp yarns are almost entirely visible on the surface of the fabric; therefore, a satin stripe is rendered by completely omitting the filling stippling on a warp painting (figures 7–19, 7–20). An entire warp stripe can be shown as a satin, or certain sections of the warp can be rendered as a satin with other stripes stippled as a plain weave. In this case, the warp stripe must be masked accordingly during stippling, so that when one filling stripe is exposed, the desired satin warp section (which is to remain unstippled) is likewise masked.

A twill weave, due to its construction, produces diagonal lines in the fabric. Once the warp of a twill stripe is painted, a ruling pen is used to mark parallel diagonal lines approximately 1/16" apart across the face of the stripe (figure 7–21). A twill plaid would be painted in the same manner except that it would be necessary to paint each filling stripe individually, using the required gouache color in the ruling pen for each section.

An iridescent solid is achieved by crossing a warp with a filling of a very close color or any opposite color while using yarns of approximately the same weight. This is painted by stippling a solid filling over a solid warp of the desired colors. For example, a deep purple warp could be crossed with a deep blue filling or with a yellowish-gold filling. Either combination would yield a fabric appearing almost solid but changing color at different angles and under different lights.

In an end-and-end stripe, warp yarns alternate in color. This would be painted, for example, with a black-and-white end-and-end stripe, by painting the warp section solid white with a brush, then drawing fine, closely spaced parallel black lines

Figure 7–19
Satin stripe, gouache on paper.
(© *N.J. Cohen*)

Figure 7–20
Plaid version of satin stripe in fig.
7–19, gouache on paper. (© *N.J.
Cohen*)

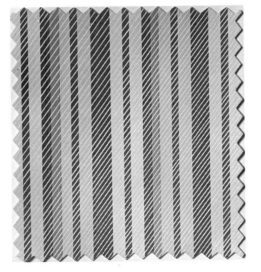

Figure 7–21
Twill stripe version of satin stripe in
fig. 7–19, gouache on paper. (© *N.J.
Cohen*)

over the white space. This yields the look of alternating black and white threads. In an end-and-end stripe the filling must be drawn with a ruling pen, producing fine, closely spaced parallel lines. If the filling in this black-and-white stripe were to be solid white, for example, the white filling would not show where it crossed the white ends but would show as a fine line crossing the black ends, thus duplicating the actual look of an end-and-end fabric. Again, as with satin stripes, end-and-end stripes may be used as sections of a design, or as a complete overall design.

It should be noted that many of the techniques used in painting yarn-dyed designs can also be used in print designs. Stippled airbrush effects excellently produce shading in prints. Any straight lines to be reproduced through printing should be drawn with a ruling pen, as they are in painted renderings of yarn-dyes. Again, although basic principles of textile fabrication and production must always be considered, all techniques can be used for further experimentation to develop new and different designs for printed and yarn-dyed fabric.

A special trick can be used to enlarge a stripe layout while maintaining the established proportion. A straightedge of the new desired repeat length is placed across the established stripe layout at such an angle that one end of the straightedge exactly meets the lower side of the repeat and the other end exactly meets the upper edge of the repeat (figure 7–22). The points at which the stripe boundaries in the original layout meet the straightedge are marked on the straightedge. A new measurement, with intervals of equal proportion to the original stripe intervals, is produced in this way. The process can

Figure 7–22
A straightedge, the length of the new desired repeat length, is laid across the existing stripe layout so that one end meets the top boundary and the other end meets the bottom boundary. The straightedge is marked at the points where it meets each stripe. In this manner, the straightedge now represents a stripe configuration of the exact proportions of the original.

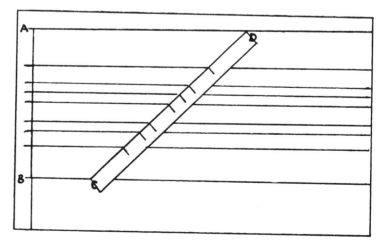

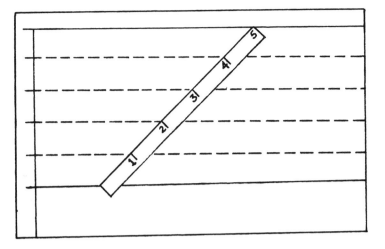

Figure 7-23
A rectangle is divided into stripes of equal widths by placing a ruler across the space so that a length of the desired number of units exactly meets the top and bottom boundaries of the rectangle. Each unit is marked along the straightedge, and a T-square is used to draw parallel lines at these points.

be reversed to reduce a stripe layout; that is, a straightedge marked with the established stripe intervals is laid diagonally between two parallel lines spaced at the interval of the new desired repeat size. The intervals are marked across this space, and a T-square is used to draw lines across the points.

A version of this technique can be used to divide a space equally into a desired number of intervals. Two parallel lines, any distance apart, can be divided into five equal parallel spaces—for example, by placing a ruler across the space. One end of the ruler is placed on the bottom line, and the ruler is angled so that the 5″ mark meets the top parallel line (figure 7–23). Each inch mark on the ruler is marked where it falls on the space to be divided; then a line is drawn through each point and parallel to the original boundaries. If the original boundaries were too far apart for the 5″ rule, 10″, 15″, or any multiple of five can be used and marked at every other inch, or every third inch, as necessary.

Designing for Jacquards

A Jacquard loom is equipped with a special head mechanism that holds and operates a set of punched cards according to the motif desired (figure 7–24). Although it is not strictly necessary that every designer understand the details of the mechanism, a weaving designer will certainly be interested and will quite easily understand the loom in action. Essentially, the warp ends are raised according to corresponding punched holes in the cards (figure 7–25). The large repeats of Jacquard fabrics allow the elaborate, intricate designs that, in this country, are produced almost exclusively for use in uphol-

123

Figure 7–24 *(above left)*
Loom with Jacquard head. The Jacquard machine above the loom allows many warp threads to be lifted individually so that the intricately patterned fabric on the loom can be woven. The Jacquard loom's harnesses (the strings that extend from the Jacquard head down into the loom) are the means by which warp threads are lifted.

Figure 7–25 *(above right)*
A close view shows different threads being lifted across the width of the loom.

stery (figure 7–26). The repeat size of the Jacquard is predetermined by the mill producing the fabric and is dependent upon both the maximum number of threads that can operate independently, and the density of the threads.

Since a warp once set in a Jacquard loom is rarely changed, the warp color is constant; and, as with any weaving, the filling can be changed more easily. Color is thus largely introduced into the Jacquard fabric through the filling.

Jacquard fabrics are often designed by drawing a print design using the required repeat size of the Jacquard. The designer then choses different weaves, perhaps from the mill's library of weaves, to be imposed into each motif area of the print design. For example, the ground area may be a satin weave, the inside sections of a flower a warp twill, the outer section of the flower a weft twill, and the leaves a plain weave. The different weaves thus yield different textures and a different proportion of warp to filling color.

Alternatively, a print design may be sent to a mill's technical staff to be translated into a weave design. In this case the successful development of the fabric is incumbent upon the technician rather than the fabric designer.

Qualifications for the Jacquard designer include sound drawing and design ability as well as a thorough understanding of fabric structure. The same standard weaves used in any woven fabric comprise Jacquard fabrics; but because it is not a shaft loom, a change in weave can be made at any point.

124

Larger, figured motifs are possible, made simply by a series of different weaves fitted together (figure 7–27). The flat pattern design (sometimes called a *cartoon*) should be used as a framework for color and motif (figure 7–28), but the quality of the fabric depends most upon the weaves, yarns, and construction. Fine detail is provided by the weaves in the cloth; therefore simplicity and boldness are most important in the cartoon. The intricacy of pattern depends upon the specific yarns and warp available; and these materials should be evaluated, perhaps in hand sample experimentation, before the Jacquard design is developed. The scale of the design must be adaptable to the scale of the weaves and fabric quality available.

Before the actual design is begun, as with most designs, the sketch of the Jacquard design should be evaluated showing side and bottom repeats. Once the cartoon is complete, the weave plan must be drawn on *point paper* (figure 7–29), which is a type of graph paper available in large sheets with different numbers of squares per inch marked off. Again, the proper

Figure 7–26
Aubusson tapestry pattern, cotton Jacquard woven fabric. (© *Craftex Mills of Pa.*)

Figure 7–27
Carmen, floral pattern, rayon/cotton Jacquard woven fabric. (© *Weave Corp.*)

Figure 7–28
Cartoon, (sketch), from which fabric in fig. 7–27 was developed. (© *Weave Corp.*)

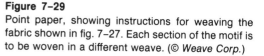

Figure 7–29
Point paper, showing instructions for weaving the fabric shown in fig. 7–27. Each section of the motif is to be woven in a different weave. (© *Weave Corp.*)

scale of point paper is chosen by its compatibility with the desired fabric structure. The compatible scale allows the point paper design to show on the paper the approximate scale the woven pattern will have. For example, if the number of warp threads per repeat is evenly divisible by twelve, it makes sense to use a point paper with twelve divisions per inch. Likewise, if the repeat is divisible by eight, an eight-ruled paper would be appropriate. If the fabric will have the same number of ends and picks per inch, the paper should have equal rules per inch in both directions. If there are many more ends than picks per inch, a comparable paper should be used.

The number of squares equal to the number of ends in one repeat must next be counted across the top of the chosen point paper and marked off. Likewise, the number of picks must be counted down the left side. The designer must then adjust the cartoon to his measurement by drawing another version of this size on tracing paper before it is transferred to the point paper.

The enlarged design is traced in pencil onto the point paper. Next, the weaves are painted in. Traditionally, this has been done in vermillion watercolor with a fine brush; but it is now

126

Figure 7-30
Ardennes, floral, cotton Jacquard woven fabric. Different weaves are used to delineate different portions of the motif, yielding a complete pattern. (© *Weave Corp.*)

Figure 7-31
Floral, cotton/rayon Jacquard woven fabric. Twills of different directions, utilizing different colors, contrast against a solid ground to achieve the design. (© *Craftex Mills of Pa.*)

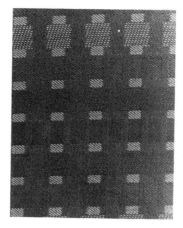

Figure 7–32
Flamestitch pattern, Jacquard woven
cotton/rayon fabric. (© *Craftex Mills
of Pa.*)

Figure 7–33
Cavendish, geometric, Jacquard woven wool fabric. (© *Boris Kroll Fabrics, Inc.*)

Figure 7–34
Floral pattern, Jacquard woven cot-
ton/rayon fabric. (© *Craftex Mills of
Pa.*)

Figure 7–35
Simulated *ikat /chiné* effect, Jacquard
woven cotton/rayon fabric. (© *Craftex
Mills of Pa.*)

usually done in pencil, then marked over with a permanent ink fine-point marker.

The weaves are drawn, not from one corner across the design, but working all areas at once to see that the weave areas will fit together. Care must also be taken that weaves join properly on each side of the repeat. Also, it is important to make sure that no long vertical or horizontal floats occur where two weaves meet.

In any weave draft, paint (or marker) usually indicates warp thread up; exposed paper indicates filling thread up. On occasion, however, the weave may be designated in some other way. It is therefore necessary to specify; and because the holes that will be punched (or cut) in the cards will indicate warp threads to be lifted, the design is usually marked, for example, "cut black" when black marks the warp threads, "cut paper" when exposed paper represents the warp threads.

Figure 7–36
Tides, geometric, Jacquard woven wool fabric. (© *Boris Kroll Fabrics, Inc.*)

When a large area features one weave, it is also common for the designer simply to color that area in with pencil and write a "key"; that is, to draw one repeat of the desired weave and instruct that it should be used for the entire penciled area.

Technology has so progressed that many mills need not draw out entire drafts on point paper. With computers, large areas of a design can be directly translated from the cartoon to the punched cards. Developments in textile design using computers are relatively slow in coming into popular use. It is therefore important that designers understand traditional practices in these matters. Figures 7–37 and 7–38 illustrate the mechanisms of a Jacquard loom.

Many, many more involved directions may be required to obtain a desired Jacquard design or to meet the stipulations of the mill involved. The specifics of every case vary, and only through individual dealings and experience can these design problems be solved. This discussion should serve as a general guideline; the designer's overall aim must be to find new ways to incorporate and draft new fabric structures. Several examples of Jacquard fabrics, showing juxtaposition of woven structures to achieve interesting surface pattern design, are shown in figures 7–30 through 7–36.

Computer-Aided Design

Nowadays computers are used in the development of fabric design, and especially in the area of woven fabrics. Computer-generated artwork does not produce as accurate a rendering of the design as is required by the engraver and print plant, but is highly useful to evaluate more quickly the various colorways

129

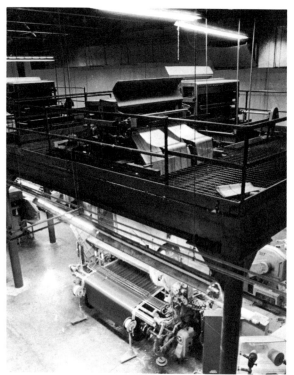

Figure 7-37
Loom with Jacquard head viewed from above (the head mechanisms may be reached from the gantry).

Figure 7-38
The punched holes in the Jacquard paper instruct the loom which harnesses to lift in sequence.

of a print design. This practice will continually increase as computer systems become more sophisticated, easier to use, and less expensive.

Yarn-dyed stripes and plaids for end uses that require limited surface effect, likewise, can be quickly simulated through computer technology. In such areas as men's shirting most companies of any size use computer artwork to cut back to a minimum the number of samples that need to be actually woven in trial blankets.

For easily and efficiently drafting basic and dobby weaves, much software is available in very simple packages for beginning weavers. In addition, computer hook-ups to hand looms that act as dobbyheads (controlling the harness lifting of the loom) are commonly used in hand-sample studios.

Computers have had the most profound impact for Jacquard fabric developments. Many looms are controlled through computer disks that directly "instruct" electronic Jacquard heads, rendering obsolete the punch paper that formerly controlled the lifting mechanism of the loom. (Plenty of punch-paper-controlled heads will probably be in use for many years to come, in which case the computer creates the punch paper.)

Jacquard designs are usually created through a combination of a drawn or painted surface pattern design to which different weaves are "plugged in." The painting or drawing is scanned in to the computer, and then the weaves are inserted, thus eliminating the need for point paper on most designs. Editing can be done to simplify weave areas or to properly join weaves, which remains time consuming but vastly more efficient than any hand method for the same process. Small designs or those with intricate joins of weaves in tight, small areas are still most efficiently handled by directly writing out a point-paper draft by hand.

Designers welcome the increased use of computers in this field; computers seem to increase the customers' demands for more designs. The more quickly we can try out more new designs, the more new product we can develop!

Color Considerations in Textile Design

8

As previously discussed, one aspect of designing for textiles differs from almost any other product design: the design is developed to be repeated across lengths and widths of fabric. Additionally, the way that fabric is colored differs from that of most other designed products: any textile pattern will be offered on the market in more than one color combination (figure 8–1).

Whereas an illustration for a book is complete once the original colorway is drawn, and a room interior is finished using only one specific group of colors, textile designs must be developed in three or four equally appealing color combinations. One floral pattern may be printed, for example, in a blue combination, a red combination, and a green combination. Besides, although each of these combinations shows a different group of colors, it is usually desirable that the alternative

Figure 8–1
In the apparel industry, fabrics are shown to customers as "types," such as the one shown here, which feature a large sample of the fabric for pattern and hand, and smaller samples of the available colorways.

combinations have similar color "feelings"; that is, the group of colors must maintain a corresponding hue relationship and have corresponding *values* (the light and dark quality of a color) and *intensities* (brightness or dullness). Such "equivalent" color groups are said to *weigh in* and are called *color combinations*. Such terms as colorway, color look, or coloring may refer to color groups that weigh in or, more generally, to any alternative color rendition of a design.

The availability of various colorways in a particular pattern allows the fabric customer ease in coordinating the fabric with other items required for a project—perhaps other fabrics, paint colors, or furniture finishes that have already been chosen for a room interior. Especially in the apparel area, color combinations must be available to the fabric customer buying several combinations of the same fabric in order to offer his product (clothing) in a choice of colors. Also, for ease in designing, he may require that the print coordinate with another group of fabrics. For example, the sportswear manufacturer may offer a jacket in navy blue, burgundy, and dark green—three hues with approximately equal intensity and value. He will then choose a print for a dress that is available in three combinations to correspond with the three jackets. The dresses, like the jackets, must maintain similar overall looks although they are different colors.

Even when such specific coordination of fabrics is not a consideration, unless colors weigh in, a change in the colors of a pattern may obviously change the look of the design. This presentation is not usually desirable because the differences may seem confusing. However, if such dramatic differences in color look *are* offered in one pattern, they may be completely separated and shown as two different fabric designs.

Techniques of Forming Color Combinations

From the start of the design process a design may be developed in more than one colorway; most often, however, one color is developed initially and others are later selected to be used in the patterns. When such combinations are designed to weigh in, a general method is followed.

First, a list is made of the colors in the original design (sometimes called the document colorway, especially if the design was developed from an actual document). The colors in the design are listed in order of prevalence in the design. As an example, the document colorway could feature a blue blotch, green as the second most prevalent color, violet as the third, accents of light orange, and small amounts of light red-orange. These colors are then located on a color wheel (figure 8–2).

By moving each color one step clockwise, the designer effects a new combination having the same hue relationship as the original. (This step need only move to the next group of primary and secondary colors. Considering tertiary colors is unnecessary detail for this procedure.) In the new group, the blotch color will be violet, the second will be blue, the third will be red, accents will be of yellow, and the smallest amounts will be of yellow-orange. Continued around the color wheel, this process yields six equivalent combinations based on primary and secondary colors.

In addition to these color groups, neutral combinations are usually considered. A cool neutral ground, like a gray or black, works very much like a blue in the design and may therefore be developed from choices I or II on the color wheel. A brown ground, being a warm neutral, would take the place of a red or orange in the design, and could therefore be adapted from choice IV. These procedures make available seven combinations showing the same hue relationship as the original (figure 8–3).

As a general rule, a printed textile will be offered in at least three color combinations: a warm, a cool, and a neutral. In the example used, the original colorway was made up largely of cool colors. The warm choice might be alternative III from the color wheel. Either neutral combination could be chosen. The combinations to be used should give as much choice to the potential buyer as possible, and no two combinations should be too similar in appearance. Fabric printing is too expensive for a company to manufacture two color combinations that are very similar, and choices that are too similar are confusing to customers.

After the alternate hue relationships are established from the color wheel and the best candidates chosen, the colors must be mixed to paint the color combinations. At this stage, each color must be developed to correspond in both value and intensity to the color in its position in the original design. This is not a precise, scientific procedure. Corresponding colors

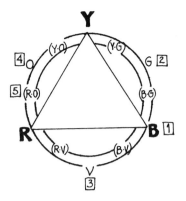

Figure 8–2
This color wheel shows the location of the colors used in the example for discussion. Locating the colors in a design on the color wheel is the first step in forming color combinations.

Figure 8–3
This chart shows the possible color choices that have corresponding hue relationships to the original design in our example.

	ORIGINAL I	II	III	IV	V	VI	COOL NEUTRAL	WARM NEUTRAL
1	BLUE	VIOLET	RED	ORANGE	YELLOW	GREEN	GRAY (BLACK)	BROWN
2	GREEN	BLUE	VIOLET	RED	ORANGE	YELLOW	BLUE	RED
3	VIOLET	RED	ORANGE	YELLOW	GREEN	BLUE	RED	YELLOW
4	ORANGE	YELLOW	GREEN	BLUE	VIOLET	RED	YELLOW	BLUE
5	RED-ORANGE	YELLOW-ORANGE	YELLOW-GREEN	BLUE-GREEN	BLUE-VIOLET	RED-VIOLET	YELLOW-ORANGE	BLUE-GREEN

must be judged together, and adjustments must be made to give the colors equal weight. At this point, as color combinations are viewed together, corresponding colors that weighed in when compared only to one another may appear slightly out of kilter. Further changes, therefore, must be made, even if these changes diverge from the results of the rotation around the color wheel.

It is important that as the colorings are developed they are periodically viewed from a distance of several feet. Close color relationships are often appealing at a close distance; but when viewed from afar, the difference may not even be noticeable. The cost of two screens will not be justified for two colors in a design that appear the same from a distance.

Note that since yellow is the lightest color on the color wheel and violet is the darkest, these two colors (especially yellow) can never weigh in as well as others. It is wise to avoid using yellow or violet in major areas of a design that must weigh in. It would be impossible to make a yellow that is the same value as a blue of equal intensity. Therefore, in using yellow or violet, the designer must manipulate the colors to give the feeling and look that are desired.

Through working, viewing the design, changing, and adapting, designers learn to develop new colorings that maintain the feeling of the original but are not so close in color as to be repetitive. Although the steps outlined here to achieve such excellence in coloring are not precise formulas, they serve as commonly used guidelines leading to the desired result.

Changing Color Looks

Although, in apparel, colorways most commonly weigh in, decorative colorways often do not strictly follow these rules but tend to emphasize the same aspects of the design throughout the color variations. However, color may also be used to change a pattern completely. This is commonly done when an old, successful pattern is resurrected by a company. The colors from years before may look quite dated, yet the pattern is completely salable. A home furnishings design may be recolored and used in apparel, as is frequently done when William Morris's designs are rendered in the purples, pinks, and greens popular for women's wear in a particular season. A conservatively colored pattern may be brightly painted for a swimwear fabric, or vice versa.

Fabrics may also be colored in such a way that some similarity is maintained even if the colorways do not weigh in. For example, an ombre could be colored in a bright version, a grayed version, and a pastel version, all with corresponding hue relationships.

A multicolor pattern is also commonly recolored as a monotone or two-color print (figures 8–4, 8–5). This effect often produces a viable pattern that not only looks quite different from the original but also is less expensive to produce because fewer screens are needed.

Presentation of Color Combinations

Once all colors have been mixed and trials made, all colors to be used in the new color combinations are selected, and a small portion of the original design is painted in each new color combination. The upper left corner, or any section that is square with the original design and will show all colors in their overall proportion, can be used to show these colorways. The coloring must be rendered in exactly the same way as the original—same paper, same transfer method, flat areas flat, dots equally dense. In the printing of fabric, each color represents a screen (or roller) that will deliver the color to the fabric in the same way each time, no matter what color is used.

Figure 8–4 *(below left)*
Floral, multicolor version of fig. 8–5, gouache on paper. (© *N.J. Cohen*)

Figure 8–5 *(below right)*
Floral, monotone version of fig. 8–4, dye on waxed *masa* paper. (© *N.J. Cohen*)

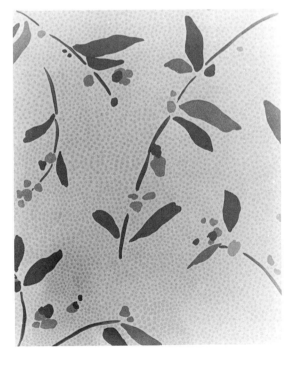

Figure 8–6
For presentation, a textile design is usually mounted on a board with its color combinations as in the illustration.

Color tabs, small square chips that show each individual color used in the design, are attached to each coloring. They may be arranged sequentially from light to dark horizontally, or sequentially from most prevalent to least prevalent color in the design. The same order should be used for each color combination so that corresponding color chips represent corresponding sections of the design.

Designers often keep swatches of color chips for reference files, and the "recipe," listing the names of tube colors used to mix the color, is written on the back of each color chip. Recipes of colors used should always be written on the back of a design. The artist may be asked to design a coordinate for the pattern, and these recipes save time in mixing colors previously used. Additionally, if a design is sold and the customer has the design put in repeat but maintains the original colorway, the recipes are a simple courtesy that saves the repeat artist time and aggravation.

When a croquis is mounted on a board for presentation, the colorings are usually mounted below the croquis on the same board (figure 8–6). If there is not room on the board for the colorings, they may be mounted together on a separate board. Color combinations for decorative designs, which are not usually mounted, are clipped to the top left corner of the design.

138

Techniques for Repeats

9

As previously discussed, textile designs are developed in such a way that along the entire length of the fabric one unit of the design will be repeated, side by side and end to end (figure 9–1). The size of these repeat units varies, depending on the width of the fabric, the type of printing, and the machinery used for the printing.

Upholstery fabrics are almost always 54″ wide, and a half-width (27″) is the measurement on which most furniture cushions are based. (Because the selvedges are not usable fabric, fabric widths are measured from within the selvedges.) The selvedges and vertical middle of the goods become seam areas and edges of furniture cushions, therefore motifs are not usually centralized on these portions of the fabric (figure 9–2). Because upholstery fabric widths are standard, they can be designed in a 27″-wide repeat. For fabric manufacturers, these repeats are usually square (that is, 27″ vertically and horizontally) because this size fits furniture easily; however, more expensive home furnishing fabrics often use 36″ vertical repeats.

Figure 9–1
El Dorado, Perricholi, and *Verrey,* Peruvian-inspired designs by Edith de Lisle, printed on cotton. (© *Lee Jofa, photograph courtesy Lee Jofa*)

Figure 9–2
Ming Trellis, floral design in layout for home furnishings upholstery. The fabric is split lengthwise down the middle to fit seating cushions. The motifs, therefore are centered down the middle of each half, and the lengthwise center axis is relatively vacant of motifs, since it will be the edges and seams of the cushions. (© *Jay Yang Designs Ltd.*)

Drapery fabrics, likewise, are of a standard width. The goods are almost always 48″ wide, and designs are developed in a 24″ horizontal repeat. The vertical repeat is often the same length.

For apparel fabrics, repeat sizes can vary tremendously not only because fabric widths may be from 36″ to 60″ but because any printing method can be used. Textile designs intended for apparel are most often designed in croquis form, to be sized later into the repeat required for a specific project. Usually the repeat will measure approximately 14″ to 16″ vertically and horizontally will be any size that divides evenly into the fabric width.

Other products have specific repeat sizes for specific end uses. For sheeting fabrics in the United States, for example, repeat sizes are usually 36″ square; and engineered patterns are also common for sheets. Pillowcases may be engineered, may be the same fabric as the companion sheets, or may be an adaptation of the sheeting pattern that is mirrored so that the pattern is "right side up" no matter which side of the pillow faces up. Towels are not designed in repeat but are so engineered that focal points appear interestingly when the towel is folded. Towel sizes vary greatly from company to company.

Repeat sizes can also be a smaller dimension dividing evenly into the required repeat size. For example, a very small-scale, all-over floral could be developed as a 4″ repeat when a 12″ roller or screen is being used. The repeat size need only be large enough to accommodate the motifs desired in the layout; designing a larger size than necessary only makes extra work for the artist. No matter how small, however, the design unit must fit, firstly, an even number of times across the width of the goods to be printed, and, secondly, an even number of times into the machinery to be used. A design with a 12″ vertical repeat will not fill a 16″ copper roller without adaptation.

The unit of the required dimensions may repeat on the fabric in a number of ways, but *half-drop repeats* are most common. In a half-drop, the repeat unit repeats directly above and below itself, but at the side the new unit is dropped down so that its top edge meets at the center of the first unit (figure 9–3). *Straight* (or block) *repeats,* in which the unit repeats directly above, below, and to the side, are also widely used (figure 9–4).

Five-star repeats, which are produced as a straight repeat, feature a large motif in the center of the repeat unit with a quarter of the motif appearing at each corner of the unit.

It should be noted that, when a 27″ half-drop repeat is used on a 54″ upholstery fabric or when a 24″ half-drop repeat is used on a 48″ drapery fabric, the two vertical halves of the fabric will differ. Usually this is not a problem; two lengths of drapery fabric are usually sewn together to form a drapery, and upholstery fabric is usually cut to 27″ squares to fit furniture cushions. Sometimes, however, it may be preferable that when the fabric is split in the warp direction the two halves be identical. In this case, the horizontal repeat size must be half the usual size.

Metrification

Fabrics produced in countries other than the United States are usually measured according to the metric system. Common apparel widths are usually produced in widths of 110 cm,

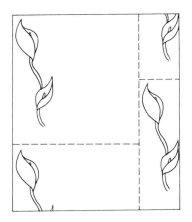

Figure 9–3
In a half-drop repeat, the unit repeats directly above and below itself. On the side, however, the unit is dropped to the midpoint of the vertical repeat length.

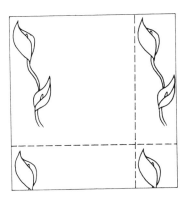

Figure 9–4
In a straight, or block, repeat the unit repeats directly above, below, and to the sides.

120 cm, 130 cm, 140 cm, or 150 cm, roughly corresponding to 43″, 47″, 51″, 55″, and 59″ respectively. Horizontal metric repeat sizes can be any evenly divisible unit of the fabric width, although upholstery repeat sizes are usually 70 cm and drapery repeat sizes usually 60 cm, corresponding with American practice. Vertical apparel repeat sizes vary. Because European sheets, towels, and pillowcases are manufactured in completely different sizes from those available in the United States, metric equivalents of repeats used in domestic products are unimportant to American textile designers, since they are rarely, if ever, involved in such projects.

The chart on page 142–143 outlines repeat sizes for specific uses measured in English and metric units. This is intended *only* as a guideline. Many factors cause deviation from these measurements: each company's equipment varies, copper rollers become worn down, new problems arise with fabric for every end use. Consistencies regarding repeat sizes are truly the exception.

CHART FOR REPEAT AND FABRIC SIZES

FABRIC USE	TYPE OF PRINTING	AMERICAN REPEAT SIZE		METRIC REPEAT SIZE		TYPICAL WIDTH OF FABRIC	
		Vertical	Horizontal	Vertical	Horizontal	American	Metric
Upholstery (primarily for decorative industry)	Flat bed screen	27″	27″	90–120 cm Larger size possible with fewer colors	70 cm	54″	140 cm
	Rotary screen	25¼ 27 36	27″	64 cm 72 cm 92 cm	70 cm		
	Heat transfer	18 23⅝ 31½	27″	46 cm 60 cm 80 cm	70 cm		
Drapery (primarily for contract industry)	Rotary screen	25¼ 27 36	24″	This width not commonly printed in Europe		48″	Width not commonly used in Europe for this industry

CHART FOR REPEAT AND FABRIC SIZES *(Continued)*

FABRIC USE	TYPE OF PRINTING	AMERICAN REPEAT SIZE		METRIC REPEAT SIZE		TYPICAL WIDTH OF FABRIC	
		Vertical	Horizontal	Vertical	Horizontal	American	Metric
Apparel	Flat-bed screen	Rarely used in USA		90–120 cm Larger size possible with fewer colors	Any size evenly divisible into width of fabric	36″ 44–45″ 48–50″ 55″ 60″	110 cm 120 cm 130 cm 140 cm 150 cm
	Rotary screen	25¼ 27 36	Any size evenly divisible into width of fabric	64 cm 72 cm 92 cm	″		
	Engraved roller (rarely used)	≈14–16″ roller becomes slightly smaller each time it is burnished down and re-engraved	″	40–42 cm roller becomes slightly smaller each time it is burnished down and re-engraved	″		
	Heat transfer	18 23⅝ 31½	″	46 cm 60 cm 80 cm			

Repeat sizes for specific uses such as sheets, towels, pillowcases, and scarves vary between manufacturers and are often engineered.

The American sizes/metric sizes may not be exactly equal. Rather, they are customarily used sizes for the same printing methods in the different systems of measure. Also, exceptions to these rules are as common as the rules themselves. (For reference: 1″ = 2.54 cm.)

Repeat sizes as given above refer to the maximum possible size for the specific use and equipment. Any smaller size that is evenly divisible into the number given is also possible. For example, with a 27″ screen, 13½″ & 7¾″ are common design repeats.

Putting the Finished Croquis in Half-Drop Repeat

Once the finished croquis is chosen or bought for a specific project, it must be put into the required repeat size. Because the croquis is usually smaller than the desired repeat size (assuming that there are no design problems with the croquis), it can simply be extended so that the whole design need not be redrawn.

143

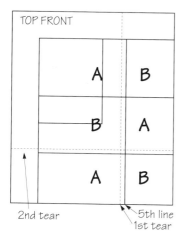

TOP FRONT

A B

B A

A B

2nd tear   5th line
                  1st tear

Figure 9–5
The drawing shows the format for putting a croquis (the shaded rectangle) into repeat, as explained in the text.

A croquis can be checked in one of two ways to see whether the design will be satisfactory in repeat. One method is to tape together along adjoining edges two small mirrors and place them facing each other at one corner of the design perpendicular to the design surface. The pattern reflected in the mirrors will approximate the repeated image.

Alternatively, a device called a repeat glass is available at some stores that carry items made of plastic. When held over the pattern, it will make the design appear smaller and show it several times next to and above itself. The image will be slightly blurred and out of focus, but layout flaws may be easily noticed with this tool.

If the croquis has no apparent flaws, a procedure can be followed to extend it systematically to the size of the repeat unit. (See format as shown in figure 9–5.)

First, the original croquis is wrapped in tracing paper for its protection and so it can be marked with instructions. Since it will be handled considerably during this process, wrapping is especially important for fragile artwork.

Next, a second piece of tracing paper is marked with a rectangle the size of the desired repeat. The boundaries of this rectangle should be extended for several inches to the right and below, and ample margins should be allowed on all sides. An axis line is drawn across the middle of the rectangle, equal distance from the top and bottom boundaries, and extending past the right boundary of the rectangle. As with all layouts, "Top Front" is marked in the upper margin. The wrapped croquis is placed under this tracing paper, its upper left corner aligned with the upper left corner of the layout.

Using a straightedge, the artist next tears the tracing paper about 1/2″ (1 cm) to the left of the right boundary of the rectangle (called the "fifth line") in order to be able to move this entire right section of the tracing paper. The "Top Front" of this tracing paper should also be marked for orientation.

Again, with a straightedge, the main tracing paper should next be torn about 1/2″ (1 cm) above the bottom boundary of the rectangle.

With a soft pencil, the croquis is lightly traced on the main piece of tracing paper, the top left hand corners aligned. Next, the original design is put aside, and the tracing paper that was torn from the bottom of the main piece is placed over the tracing just made, with right angles aligned. The motifs are in this manner traced onto the lower section, and the section is then taped (with transparent tape) back onto the edge from which it was torn.

The right panel of tracing paper, which was torn, is next

144

placed over the main tracing. However, instead of the top left angles, the next lower angle on the loose tracing paper is aligned with the top left angle of the main tracing. The motifs are traced, and in this manner the unit is "dropped" to the half-way axis of the original unit. The lower half of the original tracing is traced onto the upper half of the loose tracing paper. Once all motifs are traced, the loose tracing paper is taped back into its original position.

At this point, the motifs that appear in the upper left section (labeled "A" in the illustration) also appear below the bottom boundary and to the right of the right boundary in the middle section. In all other sections (labeled "B" in the illustration) the lower half of the croquis appears. This repeat produces a checkerboard effect of alternating sections.

Drawing with the soft lead pencil, the artist continues to extend the motifs, so that they are "filled in" to "flow" the design together in the empty spaces near the repeat unit boundaries. These areas are sometimes called the *L* or *no man's land*. As always, the design is checked from all directions for line-ups and alleyways.

Once all motifs are placed properly, the three pieces of paper are untaped; and where motifs have been changed to fit together, corrections are made. The papers can then be permanently taped in their original positions.

The motifs must next be accurately drawn. This may be done on the same piece of tracing paper, simply by refining the drawing to produce a finished layout.

A color rough—spotting in color with crayon, marker, or colored bits of paper—is next done on an overlay of clean tracing paper. It is very important that color distribution be planned by viewing one repeat *plus* the adjacent beginnings of the next repeat. Color that looks correct within one unit may yield holes when viewed in the context of side and bottom repeat.

The design is finally completed either by adding on to the original croquis (called *building out* or *painting out*) or by repainting the entire design if necessary, on a new sheet of ground paper. When the extensions of the croquis are painted or the design is repainted, the motifs must be painted exactly as they appear in the croquis. Before the design is painted, the painting techniques may need to be practiced on the same type of paper as the croquis. The new design (or the painted-out version) will be the complete design, and the croquis will no longer be used. Therefore, rough approximations are not acceptable; the new design must be executed exactly as it is to appear on fabric.

145

Figure 9-6
Two papers to be spliced together are overlapped, and the line to be spliced is cut through both layers.

Figure 9-7
The two freshly cut edges to be spliced together are joined. The seam is taped on the back with small, overlapping pieces of transparent tape.

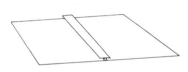

Figure 9-8
Reinforcement is added to the taped seam by rubber cementing a strip of paper over. This step is omitted when splicing *masa* paper.

Figure 9-9
The spliced line is usually cut around the edges of motifs as shown rather than as a straight line.

Splicing Paper

To add on to a croquis when it is to be put in repeat, the artist must extend the paper to continue the painting. For this purpose two pieces of paper may be spliced together to produce a semblance of a solid, larger piece of paper. Splicing can also be used, not only for repeats, but simply to produce a larger sheet than is available of a desired type of paper. Also, two different types of paper or two different techniques can be spliced to produce a desired effect.

When two sheets of paper being spliced are placed as they will be joined to form a larger sheet, the two edges to be spliced overlap slightly (figure 9-6).

The two layers are cut through, using a sharp X-Acto or mat knife.

The two thin strips removed are discarded, and the two freshly cut edges are placed together.

On the back of the paper, the newly cut edges are rubbed with a spoon or brush handle to blend them together. The splice is then taped with transparent tape (figure 9-7). Short pieces of tape should be overlapped for reinforcement; one long piece used to hold the seam will cause buckling and dimpling.

For further reinforcement a narrow strip of the same kind of paper is glued over the tape with rubber cement, applied to both the seam and the reinforcing strip, and allowed to dry before the strip is placed (figure 9-8).

In one instance this final step is omitted: with waxed or unwaxed *masa* paper, the added strip is unnecessary and would show through to the front of the design. These *masa* papers are the easiest type to splice: because they are so thin, the cut line is barely noticeable.

The cut need not be a straight line; in fact, paper is usually spliced to follow the edges of motifs (figure 9-9). Once a layout is designed, it is placed over the paper to be spliced; then a line is marked following lines of the design. By not cutting through the center of a motif or through a large ground area, the cut line attracts much less attention. Once the ground paper is spliced to the desired size, the final design is painted. In the case of painting out a repeat, the paper is spliced to the croquis and the new area painted.

146

Mill Styling

10

An additional aspect of a textile designer's job involves styling fabrics at the exact time that the initial production run is made at the mill or print plant.

A few companies locate their studios at the mill. A large mill's staff often includes a mill stylist, whose entire job is to evaluate these initial fabric runs to be sure that the fabric corresponds accurately with the original artwork on paper. Most often, however, mill styling is done by the firm's studio artists, who travel from the main office (usually in New York) to the mill (usually in a small town somewhere) on a rotation basis when it is time for new fabrics to be produced.

In printed fabric, the initial production run is called a *strike-off*. Print plants usually operate twenty-four hours a day, and necessary strike-offs are usually scheduled to begin early in the day. The night before, the designer arrives in the town

Figure 10–1
Vienna, geometric with textures, print on cotton. (© *Cyrus Clark, photograph Mikio Sekita*)

where the print plant is located so that early in the morning he can be at the plant to begin. As the fabric production on the new pattern begins, enough fabric is printed to run completely through the machine; then, a yard or two is cut off to show to the designer. A particular place with the best light available within the plant is usually designated for the designer and head printer to view the fresh fabric swatch (called a *patch*) and compare it with the artwork. Because the light in the factory is usually not good enough, it is difficult to evaluate the fabric on the print machine.

The color of the fabric is, of course, compared with the artwork for correctness of hue, value, intensity, and *fullness* (heaviness or dilution of the color). The design is checked both for *fit* (proper registration), to ascertain that motifs occur at the desired location in the design, and for quality of the *mark* (clarity and precision of desired line and shape). If other mistakes have been made in printing, such as the accidental interchanging of two colors, they must be corrected at this point.

The designer comments on adjustments that need to be made in production; then the printers go back to work and try again. In a few minutes or a couple of hours, another patch will be ready to show the designer.

The decisions must be made quickly and precisely. During this interval the print machines are stopped and waiting while the designer makes adjustments; every minute that the machines are not printing fabric costs the printing plant money. Depending on the clarity with which the designer can explain the necessary changes and the cooperation of the mill personnel, one or two patches may be enough to reproduce the artwork accurately; or many more changes may be required. Strike-offs of several patterns are usually done in one day, and the designer may be at the print plant until all hours of the night, or he may be sent back to this hotel and called to come in at an odd hour. With strike-offs, when the machines are ready the decisions must be made expertly so fabric can continue being printed and production can recommence.

It is the designer who guides the printers in producing the planned textile design. With experience, he knows what can realistically be accomplished through printing and what goals are only wishful thinking. Printing capabilities differ vastly from printer to printer and fabric to fabric. The designer's enthusiastic cooperation with the mill personnel contributes mightily toward accomplishing direct and rapid success. Mill styling (also called *mill work*) can be tiring, draining, and even boring after many hours of waiting for strike-offs; but it is almost impossible to be a successful designer without a

Figure 10-2
A loom set up with a blanket warp
shows different color sections across
the width of the warp.

thorough knowledge of this aspect of textile production. Once a designer sees firsthand what can and cannot be accomplished in printing, studio work becomes much more realistic and meaningful.

Mill styling of woven fabrics is a completely different matter. Woven stylists often spend time at the mill because familiarity with and understanding of each mill's machinery and capability is an integral part of their design work. Woven design largely involves inventing new ways to combine and use what a particular mill can do.

However, new adaptations and new colorings of woven fabrics involving changes of warps cannot be made within a matter of hours, as with prints. Therefore, woven fabrics are rarely evaluated, changed, and developed during a day at the mill. Rather, the designer submits requests to the mill and visits it to observe progress; also, samples (called *headends*) are returned to the designer for necessary changes. All this may take days of weeks, usually not hours.

However, when only filling changes are necessary, woven fabrics are often colored at the mill. Once a yarn-dyed fabric has been developed, a *blanket* is usually woven, showing all (or many) of the possible color combinations using the available yarn colors. This involves weaving samples on a *blanket warp,* which is set up on a loom with different sections of all available warp colors in the particular construction (figure 10–2). For example, if twenty warps are available in the

149

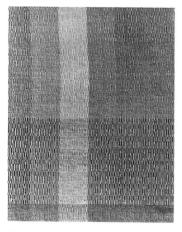

Figure 10–3

A blanket shows many color possibilities of a woven fabric by crossing alternate filling choices on the blanket warp.

specific construction, a 54" warp could be set up with approximately 2 ½" sections of each warp color arranged side by side across the width of the warp. Alternate filling choices are then tried, by sequentially weaving sections of a few inches of each choice so that each crossing of colors shows a different possibility.

Coloring fabrics in this manner is especially common in upholstery fabrics and multicolor fabrics, which are often done at the mill by a designer. (For fabrics with a solid filling color, all possible choices are usually tried.) The designer may write out many possible combinations ahead of time so the sample weavers at the mill can set up all necessary yarn colors ahead of time, setting up also the correct pattern on the loom. The designer works with the sample weaver, evaluating each combination as it is woven, making changes as required, and adding other possibilities as desired. Although this on-the-spot evaluation is much more expedient than waiting for blankets to be shipped to the studio, it is in some ways less beneficial than with printed fabrics. For example, the blanket, unlike strike-offs, cannot be cut off the loom and viewed under better light as it is produced; and the light in the weaving shed may be deceiving. Because blankets are samples and not the beginning of actual production as strike-offs are, woven coloring at the mill is a somewhat less pressured situation than print mill work.

Once the combinations are tried and the blanket is completed, it is taken off the loom and sent back to the designer at the studio (figure 10–3). The colors are cut from the blanket and evaluated, and a color line is chosen. If the designer was able to try desired possibilities at the mill, little change is necessary after the blanket is received. In this manner, much time and inconvenience is saved sending requests and samples back and forth from the mill to the studio. For both woven and printed fabric designers, mill work is and important aspect of professional performance.

Presentations of Designs

11

When a designer puts together a portfolio of work to show for job interviews, individual designs, sales, or any presentation, certain formats are customarily used.

Designs for apparel, which are usually small-sized croquis, are mounted on white Bristol board or similar stock (figure 11–1). The designs will probably vary in size, but all the mounts should be of the same size for uniformity. Two or more very small designs that were designed to go together or simply look good together may be shown on one board. With a long-reach stapler, designs are stapled to the board with one

Figure 11–1
Cornucopia, floral design, tossed layout, print on cotton. (© *P. Kaufmann, Inc., photograph Mikio Sekita*)

staple at each of the two upper corners of the design. On the back of the mount board, the staples are covered with masking tape so that they will not scratch other designs in the portfolio. When mount boards become tired and worn looking, they should be repleaced.

Designs may instead be spliced into sheets of board. This makes an attractive presentation and is much lighter when many designs are carried in a portfolio.

Color tabs may or may not be shown with croquis but usually are shown with color combinations. Color combinations are usually shown together on one board. So that each board is loose and may be easily pulled out from the group when necessary, all of the mount boards with designs are usually carried and shown in a large, black, zippered porfolio.

Because decorative designs, being much larger than apparel designs, may not fit into a portfolio when laid flat, they are not usually mounted, but are reinforced on the back of the design around the edges with a continuous strip of masking tape. The designs may be cropped to the exact boundaries of the painted design or may show the entire sheet of paper with boundaries and margins around the design. Color chips are usually shown, and designs that are in repeat are *always* shown, not only as one repeat unit but also with the beginning of the next repeat units on the right and bottom sides of the main unit. These large designs are rolled and carried in a large mailing tube, or the roll is simply covered with brown wrapping paper for hand transport.

Woven-cloth designers may either mount individual swatches on small boards or place the fabrics in a portfolio with a ring binder and vinyl-covered pages.

Once a designer has some work experience, actual fabric samples will almost always be included in the portfolio along with the artwork. The fabric is neatly folded and placed in the large portfolio or in another bag to be shown when necessary. Publicity, advertising, and other printed material showing photographs or fabric, either alone or in use, may make up a part of a portfolio. To illustrate his way of thinking during the design process, the designer may also show sketches to show ideas about the end product with swatches or croquis (figure 11–2).

Many artists develop original, attractive, and innovative ways of showing textile designs. Any presentation that not only clearly exhibits the work but also demonstrates the designer's overall personality and sense of style will only be more interesting to potential employers or customers.

Artwork intended to be sold or shown to a customer should

have a clean, neat, and precise appearance. This has been one focus of this text, but it should also be understood that a lot of textile artwork developed in studios goes directly to the engraver who prepares the screens or rollers, the artwork being purely a working record of the design. In real life, artwork does not always look perfect; on the contrary, it is done in the quickest, simplest way to accomplish the necessary results. If this artwork is later shown, any observer will appreciate the accomplished result while understanding that it was not developed to be a presentation piece.

Although it is difficult to define exactly what should be shown in a portfolio, a general guideline is that it should show both the artist's breadth of ability and his ability to develop a focused approach to one design area. To show both capabilities, the portfolio should include different types of layouts, designs (florals, geometrics, etc.), and rendering techniques as well as one or two series of designs that work together and make a "story." (See figures 11–3 and 11–4.) A variety of color looks is also important, and at least one color group that weighs in should be shown. Each artist has a particular *hand* (that is, style of drawing and rendering), but it is most desirable that an artist show designs with both a *tight* and *loose* hand (realistic, controlled and free, stylized rendering, respectively). Versatility and an ability to compose a cohesive package of designs are the traits most sought in a textile designer.

Before designs are shown to a prospective buyer, the designer should thoroughly research the company so he can show appropriate designs. Portfolios are often adjusted according to the types of customers to whom they will be shown.

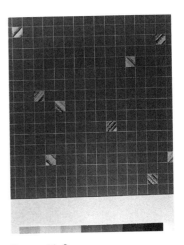

Figure 11-3
Geometric, gouache on paper. (© N.J. Cohen)

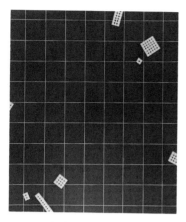

Figure 11-4
Fig. 11-3 and fig. 11-4 show two variations of a geometric on a grid ground. The two designs are a portion of a series utilizing such shapes. Geometric, gouache on paper. (© *N.J. Cohen*)

Although a portfolio may contain artwork that is several years old, it should contain nothing that looks dated or in any way problematic. A portfolio is much better with fewer pieces of the highest possible quality than with a large number that include a single piece requiring explanation and apology.

On the back of all designs should be written not only color recipes but also the repeat size, if the design is in repeat. Finally, and most important of all, for the designer's own protection the artist's name and the copyright date should be lettered prominently on the back of each piece of artwork.

Whenever possible, original artwork should be shown rather than a photostat, photograph, or color photocopy, since much of the character of the original work is lost through reproduction.

154

Professional Practices

12

The textile industry is an exciting and rewarding field for designers. However, business practices are somewhat weighted in favor of management, often to the unfair disadvantage of the design professional.

Compared with artists in other disciplines such as graphic design, illustration, and photography, textile designers traditionally receive less pay, receive credit for their work less frequently, very seldom receive royalties, pay their agents a larger percentage, and must often relinquish copyrights on their work. Most of these practices have become commonplace because of the designer's ignorance, and the almost universal acceptance of low standards makes it even more difficult for individual designers to demand what they are due.

Nowadays, however, designers are becoming much more aware of professional standards, largely through improved and increased communication among themselves. Flow of information among practicing artists of all disciplines allows standardization of pricing and of business practices.

To begin a discussion of how specific business practices should be handled is, indeed, to open Pandora's box. Although many common practices are unfair, it is difficult for any designer to stand up for principles and simultaneously maintain and develop cooperative relationships with the management of textile companies. As a designer becomes more experienced, healthy work relationships—and not rebellious, non-trusting behavior on the part of a designer—are what promote ethical standards in the industry. While the designer constantly considers his professional reputation, he must also help to establish industry-wide professional standards. The issues differ for free-lance and staff artists; but because staff artists often hire or buy from free-lancers (who are actually self-employed), the ethical questions confronted in this profession need to be understood by everyone.

The most important concern of an artist is his right to control the use of his work. As soon as a designer creates an original textile design, he has federal copyright, which lasts for the artist's life plus fifty years. Copyright is a bundle of rights, allowing artists to control separately and with specific limitations the usage of the artwork. For the artist's protec-

155

Figure 12–1
Copperplate print on cotton, English, Bromley Hall, ca. 1775. (*The Metropolitan Museum of Art, Gift of Dr. and Mrs. Roger Gerry, 1982. 2002.2*)

tion, copyright notice should be placed on all work. This notice must include copyright, copr., or ©; the artist's name or an abbreviation by which the artist is known; and the year of first publication. Furthermore, for the artist's protection, all artwork should be registered with the U.S. Copyright Office. Because unpublished work can be registered in groups, the $10 registration fee can cover, for example, all designs created by one artist during one year. All copyright registration forms and a Copyright Information Kit can be obtained at no charge from the Copyright Office, Library of Congress, Washington, D.C. 20559.

If artwork is created in the course of a designer's full-time employment, the employer has copyright of the work unless a statement has been signed to the contrary. When, however, a textile work created by a free-lance artist is printed or manufactured, the law presumes that the right to use the design for only that one designated purpose has been transferred. The copyright, which is all other rights, belongs to the creator of the work. Permission to use a design for any specific purpose should be a written and signed authorization. Written authorization is *necessary* to transfer the copyright (*all* rights to use the design).

When a client pays a fee for the rights to reproduce a textile design, he is in no way purchasing the artwork itself; nor does the purchase of the artwork (for an additional fee, for example) constitute a transfer of copyright.

Dealings between textile designers and their agents or clients have long been handled verbally and without specific stipulations.

However, for the protection of all artists, every designer should maintain written records. These include agreements with agents, permission for artwork to be held by a potential buyer for a specified time, and confirmation and invoice (billing) of every design project. When a design project is accepted, all items requested by the client should be written out, and this agreement should be signed by both the artist and the client. The transfer of any right to reproduce a design should be made in writing, and a written invoice (bill) should be sent to the client. These are simple procedures that all business people need in order to avoid misunderstandings, and to maintain permanent records.

Design fees depend on many factors, including the type and complexity of the work, the artist's reputation, and the value of the intended use of the artwork. If a buyer intends to use the work for more than one purpose, especially for more than one area of the market, he should pay more for the additional rights because the artist might otherwise have sold the design to a buyer for a different market. An artist may, for example, sell the rights to a design to one manufacturer for wallpaper and to another for sheets and pillowcases. If one buyer wants to use the work for both of these purposes, he should compensate the artist accordingly.

All of these principles are more easily stated than accomplished. Most textile design buyers are accustomed to buying

157

artwork for a flat fee, then either using the work as they please or keeping it on file, perhaps not using it at all and never returning it to the artist. This problem is compounded by studios, both European and American, that sell artwork and all rights to buyers for relatively low prices. Additionally, a buyer often purchases a croquis or design simply to use the motifs in another design, use the technique with other motifs, or otherwise change the design so completely that it would be unrecognizable as a version of the specific artwork. In this manner, buyers are accustomed to purchasing groups of croquis as studies—that is, springboards to work from—and consider any name recognition of the creator of the work to be blowing a small issue out of proportion. There are, however, laws in some states protecting an artist from having his work changed so that it is presented to the public in a distorted way.

Many buyers do not even bother purchasing designs; they simply buy a yard of fabric to adapt the pattern in one way or another. Unfortunately, the business of fabric design is often viewed, not as creation of original work, but as redoing patterns already on the market, varying the pattern only slightly to avoid copyright infringement. Designers are often asked to do knock-offs; to oblige, the artist may become liable. The converter requesting the knock-off should sign a statement accepting responsibility.

Many buyers of artwork want exclusive rights to a particular work and also want the artist to hold and not sell similar designs to any other buyers in the same market. All of these issues must be dealt with individually, depending on the artist's relationship with the client and the price involved. Artists today, however, successfully request and obtain equitable treatment from most clients.

Royalties and artist's credit (with the designer's name on the fabric's selvedge) are particularly difficult to obtain in the textile industry; but, as designers' reputations are established, these compensations are becoming more frequent.

Although simultaneous work by an artist for different, non-competitive companies is reasonable, it is frowned upon by many companies. When beginning a new project, artists are probably best off discussing openly with those involved the areas that are potentially sensitive. When everyone has been informed, uncertainties that arise later can be dealt with more smoothly.

If the artist is expected to relinquish certain income-producing projects, he should, of course, be paid accordingly by the employer making the demands.

Because textile designers are often required to travel to

mills and to work there long hours consecutively during strike-offs, these demands on the designer may became abusive. When it is requested, most designers receive compensatory time, and in some cases overtime, for mill work. Although these hours at the mill may be long, most of the time is spent waiting for fabric to be ready; and designers are usually comfortably accommodated during their wait. It should also be noted that mill work is rarely done by rank beginners; and the more experienced designer may also be required to travel not only to mills, but also to trade shows, and numerous other events. Although at times the job requirements disrupt the designer's personal life, they are no more unreasonable than travel requirements of most other professions.

Textile designers may be salaried employees of a firm, or they may be free-lance designers. Free-lance designers may be paid on an hourly basis (usually for technical work, such as handweaving or fabric analysis), on a project basis, or at a per diem rate. Rate estimates for projects are usually based on both the artist's expected per diem rate and the time the project will require. Even experienced designers find it difficult to predict the time and work requirements of a project. Estimates are made with every aspect being carefully considered; however, allowances must be agreed upon by both parties so that the designer will be compensated for changes that are required during the course of a project.

Per diem rates, rather than a salary, are sometimes paid to artists who work full-time for a company. Benefits (health insurance, vacation time) are included or financial compensation is made in order that advantage not be taken of the artist.

Unless the buyer agrees to pay for the time required for the work whether or not the work is accepted, the artist is imprudent to work on speculation.

All questions regarding pricing and ethical standards that arise during a designer's career are best evaluated in the context of the professional experience of several designers. Open communication among designers has been greatly increased through the efforts of the Graphic Artists' Guild's Textile Designers' Guild division. Although better researched for some categories of the discipline than for others, their *Pricing and Ethical Guidelines* serves as an excellent basis for any question on professional standards. The Graphic Artists' Guild maintains offices in most major cities and can be consulted for further information.

13 Green Design

A fabric designer's job has taken on new complexity. No longer does our product need only to be beautiful, hold to high design standards, and be suitable for its end use and market. Today we must also consider the environmental consequences of the manufacture and use of the products we design. Responsibility for these ramifications is surely held only in small part by the designer, but the factors need to be understood by all personnel who participate in the fabrication process. Designers may well be the inventors of new techniques and processes that will enable all fabrics to be made with safer practices that lead to cleaner land, air, and water for all of us.

To realize the environmental impact of textile manufacture, an overall view of its processes must be considered.

First, can fibers be grown or made from replenishable materials, and can they be processed in ways that use fewer chemicals? Plant fibers may seem the best choice of an environmentally friendly material, because they are natural materials themselves, and because organic agricultural production with-

Figure 13–1
Upholstery fabrics such as Polarfleece® can be made of recycled fiber. Wing Chair. (Milling Road, A Division of Baker Furniture. *Photo courtesy of Milling Road*)

out addition of synthetic chemicals is a concept familiar to most consumers. However, even synthetic fibers are produced through the use of natural resources, and responsibly produced synthetics that utilize recycled fibers, for example, may ultimately deplete fewer resources than perceived "natural" materials.

Next, how must the fiber be processed to be made into fabric, and how are color and finishes applied? Some natural fibers require no addition of color to the raw material, but color palettes derived in this manner may be narrower than the buying public desires! Sheep and alpaca naturally grow hair of black and brown and off-white; hybrid strains of cotton produce various shades of brown fiber. But the full-color palette achieved through addition of dyestuffs cannot be created through these cultivation strategies.

Nonetheless, dyestuffs vary greatly in toxicity levels, as do process-treatment facilities for water used by dye houses. As with raw fiber, "natural" dyestuff materials are not necessarily less harmful than are synthetic counterparts. People find many natural materials toxic, whether these materials touch their skin or enter their water supply.

How must a fabric be after-treated? The concerns of textile users sometimes require additional chemicals to impart characteristics of, for example, fire retardance or stain repellence to a product. All desired performance features of fabrics need to be weighed against their environmental costs.

How will a fabric be cleaned? Dry cleaning and washing have different environmental impacts.

Where is a given fabric produced, and what are the environmental concerns of its makers? In the United States there are well-established governmentally regulated standards for most manufacturing processes and facilities. Many beautiful fabrics imported to the U.S. are produced in countries with much less rigorous requirements. When we design fabrics or otherwise encourage their production in areas without green concerns, we are taking a position on environmental impact.

Can a fabric be rolled, stored, packaged, and shipped with recycled and reusable materials and supplies? While not strictly textile concerns, all these aspects relate to the overall impact.

What will be the useful life of a textile product, and how will it ultimately be disposed of? Eventually all fabrics wear out. Can reuses be found? Can the product be made into something else?

Our best green reason for supporting good design in all products is that when a product really works, its life is long.

The longer the useful lives of all the products we use, the less of it becomes garbage. An increasingly important and difficult task for all designers will be to consider the environmental consequences of their development decisions.

GLOSSARY

alleyways Unintentional lines formed by negative spaces (spaces vacant of motifs) in a design.

all-over layout A design that, within one repeat unit, has irregularly occurring motifs connected in some way.

balance A design with no line-ups, alleyways, or holes is said to be in balance.

balanced stripe A layout of stripes that is symmetrical relative to one stripe at the center of the configuration.

bayadere A horizontal stripe.

bende effect A halftone-like appearance of shading in one color, produced in screen printing by the dense or sparse spacing of dots of the desired color.

blanket A piece of yarn-dyed fabric made with sections of different warp colors crossed with sections of different filling colors so that many alternate color choices can be viewed in one fabric.

blotch A background area of a design printed in the same way the motifs are printed. Fabrics so printed are said to be blotch printed.

botanical A design showing entire plant forms rendered as in a botanical illustration.

burn-out print A fabric made of cellulosic and synthetic fibers, on which an acid is applied in certain areas to dissolve the cellulosic fibers and leave part of the fabric translucent.

chinoiserie Any Western interpretation of an oriental design.

chintz A floral pattern, usually large-scale, with strong, vibrant colors.

class of dye Category of a particular type of dye because of its affinity for a particular fiber or fibers. Fiber-reactive dyes, for example, are a class that will bond with cellulosic fibers.

color combination An alternate colorway of a textile design that weighs in to the original.

colorway, color look, or coloring Alternate color choices for a design that do not necessarily weigh in.

contemporary A design featuring simple, extremely stylized motifs.

contract The market that supplies fabric (and furniture) for commercial (non-residential) interiors such as offices, hotels, hospitals, and schools.

conversational A design using pictures of recognizable objects as motifs; also called a figurative.

163

converter A company that buys unfinished fabric, has it printed, dyed, or finished on a commission basis, and sells the finished product to another customer; also the person working for a textile company who handles the flow of goods between these processes.

coordinates Designs developed to be used together.

croquis A textile design in balance but not in repeat.

decorative The portion of the textile market that supplies fabric for upholstery, drapery, and wall covering to be used in homes; also called the home furnishing or residential market.

directional A design in which all motifs are oriented in one direction so that the design looks correct only when viewed from one direction.

discharge printing An expensive multistep printing method in which the ground cloth is dyed a solid color, desired areas are bleached out, and the bleached areas are simultaneously printed with another color.

documentary A design derived from a specific style or fabric. The original from which the design is derived is called the document.

domestics Fabrics designed and produced for sheeting, towels, blankets, and other bed, bath, or kitchen textile products.

engineered pattern A design in which one screen makes the entire, completely self-contained pattern that is used for one object such as a towel or scarf.

fall-on (trap) An effect achieved by printing one color over a different one to yield a third color. Because they are difficult to control and predict, fall-ons are not commonly used.

fiber The natural or man-made raw material of which fabrics are made (e.g., wool, cotton, silk, acrylic, polyester).

finishing Any treatment of a fabric after dyeing to set the color, to remove excess dye and sizing, to add a luster or sheen, to produce such specific effects as embossing.

flock printing Applying an adhesive to certain areas of a fabric, then dusting the fabric with fine, loose fibers that adhere to the adhesive.

foulard A small-scale pattern in which all motifs are repeated directly above, below, and next to each other (e.g., polka dots); also called a set pattern or a tailored pattern.

griege goods (grey, gray, greige) Fabric that has been woven but has not been wet- or dry-processed in any way.

ground A textile surface, either dyed or undyed, onto which motifs are printed.

halftone Gradual shading from light to dark in one color, using only one roller to achieve the effect; possible only in roller printing.

hand 1) The way a fabric feels when handled; 2) the "style" of an artist's designs. *Tight hand* indicates very fine, detailed rendering; *loose hand,* a freer, more stylized way of drawing.

head end   An initial production sample of a woven fabric, usually about a yard long, to be evaluated before further production is begun.

heat-transfer printing (sublistatic printing)   First printing the design on paper with printing inks containing dyes, then applying the paper—with heat and pressure—to fabric, transferring the dyes; possible only on certain synthetics; infinite color and shading possibilities.

holes   Uneven gaps between motifs in a design.

Jacquard   A head mechanism for a loom (also, the fabric it produces) invented by Joseph J. M. Jacquard in 1801–1804. The Jacquard machine, positioned above the loom, holds a set of punched cards that instruct the loom as to the pattern to be woven by means of punched holes corresponding to threads to be lifted.

jobber   A textile company that buys a finished product and resells the fabric, usually in smaller quantities, to another customer.

juvenile   A pattern to be used for children's clothing, linen, dishes, etc.

knock-off   A textile design produced by one company to copy a successful design of another company. Although the knock-off is usually less expensive than the original, it may all the same take business away from the original fabric. (*Knock off* as a verb refers to the act of copying.)

layout   The tracing paper plan for a textile design, showing the arrangement of motifs.

line   The group of products sold by one company and released to show to the market at one time; also called a range or collection.

line-ups   Unintentional lines formed by motifs in a design.

market   1) A segment of the textile industry that handles fabric for a particular end use, such as the apparel market, decorative market, or contract market; 2) a segment of the textile industry that sells fabric of a particular price range, such as middle market, high end of market; 3) the time of year when a particular segment of the industry introduces new product lines, usually twice a year for each segment of the industry.

mill   A company that owns the necessary equipment and uses it to produce fabric.

mill work (mill styling)   The portion of a textile designer's job that must be done at the mill (or print plant), involving, among other matters, checking for accuracy the initial production runs of fabric.

mongrel design   A plaid in which the warp stripe layout and filling stripe layout differ.

motif   A distinctive and recurring form, shape, or figure in a design.

165

ogee   A layout featuring onion-shaped motifs.

ombre   A stripe composed of distinct bands of color closely related in hue, value, or intensity and placed in graded order from lightest to darkest or dullest to brightest.

pattern   A design for decorating a surface composed of a number of elements arranged in a regular or formal manner.

piece   A bolt of fabric of the length usually woven.

piece-dyed   Fabric dyed after being woven in piece, or bolt, form, usually in a solid color.

pigment printing (dry printing)   Applying color to cloth using pigment, which unlike dye, does not interact to bond with the cloth surface but attaches with a vehicle of resin binders. The cloth is dry when it is pigment-printed, and the effect of this method is that the color appears to sit on the surface of the cloth.

point paper   A paper, similar to graph paper, onto which the thread-by-thread plan for the Jacquard design is drawn.

printing   The production of patterns or motifs on fabric by applying a coloring agent to the fabric surface in specific areas.

Provençal   Country-French textile designs, derived from eighteenth-century wood-block prints; usually small-scale, set patterns.

railroad   To turn a horizontal stripe sideways when upholstering on furniture so that the stripe is vertical.

registration (fit)   Exact alignment of all rollers or screens in order to print all motifs onto the fabric in correct relation to one another.

repeat   One standard design unit containing a specific arrangment of motifs, which is repeated across the width and along the length of a fabric. The horizontal repeat size must divide evenly into the width of the fabric to be printed.

roller printing (cylinder printing, direct printing)   A printing method similar to newspaper printing, in which fabric is fed into the machine and passed between the color rollers and the main cylinder. The rollers are made of copper, and each is engraved with the motifs that it will contribute to the complete design. A separate roller is needed for each color in the design.

rotary printing   Cylindrical "screens," made of aluminum mesh, are masked in certain areas, and dye is applied from the inside of the screen through the unmasked areas onto the fabric. A separate screen is needed for each color in the design.

screen printing   Forcing dye through unmasked areas of a silk or nylon screen stretched on a wooden frame, a process accomplished by hand, or more commonly, through automation. A separate screen is necessary for each color in the design.

side repeat   The horizontal repeat across the cloth.

striae   A stripe that changes subtly in color and/or texture throughout the fabric.

strike-off   The initial production trial made of a printed fabric so

166

that accuracy of color and design may be verified before full production begins.

stylist The person employed by a textile company to direct and coordinate the development of the company's product line.

tartan Any plaid of the bold reds, blues, greens, and yellows with black-and-white accents in balanced, sometimes true, designs, usually woven in twill or plain weave typical of Scottish tartans.

textile A woven fabric.

tjanting A penlike tool with a wooden handle and metal spout/point that is dipped into hot wax and then used to deliver the wax to areas of a fabric (or design) through the metal spout.

toile A fine-line, one-color floral or scenic pattern showing large areas of the natural ground cloth.

tossed layout A design in which motifs do not recur at regular intervals within one repeat unit.

transitional A stylized design for home furnishings, usually showing some recognizable naturalistic motifs.

trompe l'oeil Patterns designed to produce the illusion of absent architectural features or to show realistically rendered objects.

true design A plaid composed of a warp and a filling stripe that are identical.

two-dimensional stripe (three-dimensional, etc.) A stripe made up of two (three, etc.) sizes of stripes within the pattern.

vertical (vertically integrated) A textile company that performs operations on more than one manufacturing level; for example: spinning yarn, weaving, dyeing, and finishing fabric.

warp Lengthwise yarns in woven fabric.

warp printing Printing the warp of the fabric before the fabric is woven. When woven, the threads shift slightly, yielding somewhat fuzzy, indistinct edges of motifs.

weaving The interlacing of two sets of threads, one in a vertical and the other in a horizontal direction, to form a fabric.

weft Crosswise (horizontal) yarns in woven fabric.

weigh in Two groups of colors that maintain a corresponding hue relationship and have corresponding values are said to weigh in.

wet printing Printing in which the cloth to be printed is damp and is impregnated with dyes that bond chemically with the surface of the cloth.

yarn-dyed Fabric woven of yarns already dyed is said to be yarn-dyed. Striped and plaid fabrics are yarn-dyed.

BIBLIOGRAPHY

Some of the books in this list are out of print and available only through libraries and book-search services.

Albeck, Pat. *Printed Textiles*. Oxford Paperbacks Handbooks for Artists. Vol. 5. New York: Oxford University Press, 1969.

Albers, Josef. *The Interaction of Color*. New Haven: Yale University Press, 1975.

American Fabrics and Fashion Magazine, eds. *Encyclopedia of Textiles*. Englewood Cliffs NJ: Prentice-Hall, Inc., 1980.

Barker, A. F. An Introduction to the Study of Textile Design. New York: E. P. Dutton & Co., 1982.

Billcliffe, Roger. *Charles Rennie Mackintosh: Textiles Designs*. rev. ed. Pomegranate Artbooks: Rohnert Park CA, 1993

Birren, Faber. *Principles of Harmony and Contrast*. West Chester, PA: Schiffer Publishing Co., 1987.

Blum, Herman. *The Loom Has a Brain*. rev. ed. Philadelphia: Craftex Mills, Inc. of Penna., 1973.

Bury, Hester. *A Choice of Design 1850-1980*. London: Warner & Sons, Ltd., 1981.

Crawford, Tad. *Legal Guide for the Visual Artist*. New York: Allworth Press, 1995.

Dalley, Terence et al., eds. *The Complete Guide to Illustration and Design Techniques and Materials*. London: Book Club Associates, 1984.

Dan River, Inc. *Dictionary of Textile Terms*. 14th ed. New York: Dan River, Inc., 1992.

Emery, Irene. *The Primary Structures of Fabrics*. Washington, DC: The Textile Museum, 1980.

Fannin, Allen A. *Handloom Weaving Techniques*. New York: A. & D. Fannin, 1979.

Gentille, Terry A. *Printed Textiles*. Englewood Cliffs, NJ: Prentice Hall, Inc., 1982.

Graphic Artists Guild. *Graphic Artists Guild Handbook: Pricing and Ethical Guidelines*. 8th ed. New York: Graphic Artists Guild, 1994.

Gray, Bill. *Complete Studio Tips*. New York: W. W. Norton & Co., 1996.

Grimble, Ian. *Scottish Clans & Tartans*. New York: Crown Publishing, 1986.

Grosicki, Z. J. *Watson's Advanced Textile Design*. 4th ed. London: Butterworth & Co., Ltd., 1977.

Hardingham, Martin. *The Fabric Catalog*. New York: Pocket Books, 1978.

Huhenadel, P., and J. Relton. *The Modern Textile Dictionary*. Plainfield NJ: Textile Book Service, 1979.

Johnston, Meda P., and Glen Kaufman. *Design on Fabrics*. New York: Van

Nostrand Reinhold Co., 1981.

Joseph, Marjorie L. *Introductory Textile Science*. 6th ed. Orlando, FL: Harcourt Brace College Publishing, 1993.

Joyce, Carol. *Designing for Printed Textiles*. Englewood Cliffs, NJ: Prentice Hall, Inc., 1982.

——————. *Textile Designs: The Complete Guide to Printed Textiles for Apparel & Home Furnishings*. New York: Watson-Guptill Publications, Inc. 1993.

Justema, William. *Pattern*. Boxton: New York Graphic Society, 1976.

——————. *The Pleasures of Pattern*. New York: Reinhold Book Corp., 1968.

Kirby, Mary. *Designing on the Loom*. Tarzana, CA: Studio Publications, 1955.

Larsen, Jack L., and Jeanne Weeks. *Fabrics for Interiors: A Guide for Architects, Designers, and Consumers*. New York: Van Nostrand Reinhold Co., 1975.

Lubell, Cecil. *Textile Collections of the World: United States and Canada*. Vol. 1. New York: Van Nostrand Reinhold Co., 1976.

——————. *Textile Collections of the World: United Kingdom and Ireland*. Vol. 2. New York: Van Nostrand Reinhold Co., 1976.

——————. *Textile Collections of the World: France*. Vol. 3. New York: Van Nostrand Reinhold Co., 1977.

Mara, Tim. *The Thames & Hudson Manual of Screen Printing*. London: Thames & Hudson, 1979.

Marcoux, Alice. *Jacquard Textiles*. Providence, RI: Rhode Island School of Design, 1982.

Mayer, Ralph. *The Artists' Handbook of Materials and Techniques*. 5th ed. Revised and updated by Steven Sheehan. New York: The Viking Press, 1991.

Moss, Tobias, ed. *A. I. Friedman, Inc.: Quality Art and Drafting Materials*. New York: A. I. Friedman, Inc., 1994.

Parry, Linda. *William Morris Textiles*. New York: Viking Press, 1983.

Pizzuto, Joseph J. *Fabric Science Instructor's Guide*. Edited by Allen C. Cohen and Arthur Price. New York: Fairchild Books, 1990.

Rossbach, Ed. *The Art of Paisley*. New York: Van Nostrand Reinhold Co., 1980.

Storey, Joyce. *The Thames and Hudson Manual of Dyes and Fabrics*. New York: Thames and Hudson, 1992.

——————. *The Thames and Hudson Manual of Textile Printing*. New York: Thames and Hudson, 1974.

Walch, Margaret. *Color Source Book*. New York: Charles Scribners's Sons, 1979.

Watson, W. *Advanced Textile Design and Colour*. London: Longmans Green and Co., Ltd., 1947.

——————. *Textile Design and Colour*. London: Longmans Green and Co., Ltd., 1947.

Yokoo, Tadanori. *The Made in Japan Textiles of Jurgen Lehl*. Tokyo: Parco, 1983.

INDEX

MARYPAUL YATES is a principal of Yates Weisgal Inc., a textile design and sales consulting firm in New York City. She has been responsible for the creative direction and product development of numerous textile companies in the fashion and interior furnishings fields. She studied at the University of Georgia and received a BFA degree from Syracuse University and an AAS degree from the Fashion Institute of Technology in New York. She has taught at FIT and the Parsons School of Design, she lectures widely, is active in professional organizations, and is currently writing a second book.